D1727034

Darkness Disguised as Light

The Hidden Truth About Psychic Protection and the Illusion Matrix

Maya Zahira

DEDICATION

I would like to thank everyone who supported me in this journey. Just knowing you have my back means more than you know! I am deeply grateful for those who pray for me daily for strength and protection. Lastly, I would like to thank my spiritual allies who have shared their guidance over the years and held me in loving grace during the darkest nights of my soul.

CONTENTS

The details in this story are absolutely true and real, only the names, locations, and minor details have been changed to ensure the anonymity of all involved. All information in this book is based on the author's firsthand experiences.

INTRODUCTION

The Haunted Farmhouse
Exhausted, I crawled under the covers, and as soon as I laid my head onto the pillow, I began to hear what sounded like hundreds of very loud whispers. "Crap," I muttered to myself. "This place is haunted. Why didn't I check for that before I moved in?"

It was the year 2000 and I was living in a small rural parish, not far from New Orleans, Louisiana. Following my divorce the year prior, I decided it was time for a change. My plan was to create a new life for myself, to save enough money in six months so that I could move away from the city where I had been married and later divorced. In preparation for that move, I decided to save money by leaving the house I had been renting to stay in an old farmhouse outside of a small town. I went to meet Dorothy, the elderly woman who owned the home, and I saw the upstairs bedroom where I would be staying. From what I could see, it seemed like a positive situation. Dorothy needed a roommate, and the space was mine, rent-free. I moved my things into the small bedroom, but that night, when I went to bed and heard those whispers, I realized that I had made a huge mistake.

Within the next week, I began to sense several ghosts in the house. Most seemed to be fairly benign. On one occasion, I saw a petite woman in old-fashioned prairie clothing. She had long, kinky, blonde hair and was holding an infant in her arms. A ghost with long, straight, black hair also made an appearance, wearing similar clothing. Neither of them spoke, but I got the sense that there were many other ghosts within the house and that they were somehow trapped by another spirit, one that felt very, very dark and evil.

During my seventh night in the farmhouse, I suddenly awoke from a deep sleep. Opening my eyes, I saw a dark, black, shadow figure hovering above me, and I had the horrifying realization that I was having an orgasm. I felt the weight of the evil entity pressing down onto my whole body, and I could not move or speak. It had violated me sexually. I was afraid, but I was powerless, and could do nothing to stop it. I squeezed my eyes shut, and the next thing I knew, it was morning.

I got up early to get ready for work and tried to shake off the experience. I went on with my day, and by late afternoon I began to feel the dull ache and discomfort that comes on when I'm starting to get a urinary tract infection. I stopped by the grocery store and bought some cranberry juice, thinking that would do the trick. Later that night I woke up with horrible pain in my lower abdomen. I was unable to work over the next few days as I tried to heal from the UTI. I went to the doctor and started taking antibiotics. I had the suspicion that maybe it was the encounter with the dark entity that had made me sick. That was too scary to admit, so I shoved the thought to the back of my mind.

One day, when I was resting in bed trying to recover, I suddenly got chills down the back of my neck. In that instant, I heard a man's voice clearly, and loudly, whisper my name into my right ear. The voice was so eerie and malevolent. It sounded so close, as though the dark being was just an inch from my ear! After that happened, I finally admitted that I had a very real problem on my hands.

Unfortunately, I was having a hard time getting over the infection. It persisted, and I continued on a different course of antibiotics. As a result of the lengthy treatment, I developed a horrible candida (yeast) infection that started in my digestive system, and eventually spread throughout my whole body.

In the meantime, I was trying to get this dark being out of the house where I was staying. The spiritual mentors I had at the time suggested I burn sage, which I did. I was able to get some of the ghosts to move out of the house, but the dark entity would not budge. Finally, I gave myself permission to get creative, and I came up with some of my own unique ideas to tap into my power and force the evil spirit to leave. A few days later I saw the figure in the doorway of my bedroom. With every bit of mental focus I had, I visualized that I was a powerful, roaring mountain lion. I literally lunged toward the entity as I tapped into an inner power beyond my usual strength. I could feel that the being was surprised at my show of power, and it backed away to the hallway ceiling near the attic door. With one more surge of inner power I was able to get it to move up into the attic where it would no longer be cohabitating with me in my daily living space, but for the remaining time I lived there I was not able to get it to completely leave the house.

I moved out of the farmhouse about six months later and relocated to a new city. I continued to have chronic health issues that began the night I had been sexually violated by the dark being. A few months after relocating, I found a local shamanic healer who does Reiki and intuitive work. I thought, perhaps, I could get some assistance in clearing out the residual energy from what had happened to me. As I lay on the treatment table, I told him all about the evil entity from the haunted farmhouse, how my health had plummeted as a result of the attack, and that I wanted him to help clear and heal it for me. The shamanic healer just looked at me, shook his head condescendingly, and said, "No, it doesn't work like that. Ghosts cannot harm you." So, he continued the healing session, apparently balancing my aura and chakras, and I left the session with absolutely no improvement in my health.

For the next six months, I was so ill I believed I might actually die from this mysterious illness. Desperate to find help, I sought the assistance of various spiritual and holistic healers, and their response was always the same. They either did not believe me, or they did not have a clue how to help someone heal from an entity attack. In addition, I went to multiple medical doctors who were all puzzled by my health issues, which did not fit into their medical diagnosis box. I finally did receive assistance from a naturopathic physician who gave me some very good wellness protocols that helped improve my health about 25%. It ended up taking me a full five years to recover my health to 80% of what it had been before that horrifying event.

Had I been able to find someone who specialized in the impact and aftermath of entity attacks, I am certain that my physical and emotional suffering would have been greatly reduced. In fact, if the information I needed had been available at the time, I likely would not have gotten ill, and may have been able to avoid the violating encounter altogether. Years would pass before I would have another brush with the dark even more disturbing than this.

MY VOW, UNVEILED

I would like to share with you the core reasons why I have been called to step forward at this point in time and make psychic self-protection a focal point in my life's work. Recently, I was talking with one of my teachers about how, and why, I am so passionate about this aspect of my work. In a very candid and heartfelt way, I was explaining some of my past experiences with psychic attack, and how they impacted me on such a deeply emotional and spiritual level. She responded, "Maya! You absolutely need to share this! Share it just like you did with me, straight from the heart. There are so many people who need to hear this!"

And so, here I am...sharing my story. My intention is that the information in this book will come straight from my heart with vulnerability and transparency. I am not one for putting slick and shiny offerings out into the world. I prefer to be authentic and real. As I write, I'm following my inner wisdom and guidance from the Divine, and I trust that it will unfold perfectly for the people who need it most. If you're reading this book now, I believe there was a reason you were drawn to this topic, and my deepest desire is that you will receive what you need here.

I have worked as a healer and teacher for over twenty-five years, and throughout the long span of my work, I have always felt that psychic self-defense was extremely important. Over the years, I have encountered many people in the spirituality and alternative healing fields who have expressed their views on psychic protection. The prevailing comment is that psychic self-defense is not necessary, and that it is very fear-based to focus on protection of any kind. I respectfully, and strongly, disagree, and here is why: When we get into our car and we buckle the seat belt (because we are taking a prudent and reasonable safety measure), are we putting on that seat belt because we are being fear-based in our beliefs? No, we are doing it because we are being prudent. So, what about a woman or man who decides to go to a physical self-defense class at a karate studio? Is their decision to learn some physical empowerment tools necessarily fear-based? No, I don't believe so. Of course, it does depend on the person and their intentions, but I think that learning self-defense techniques is very smart. In and of itself, it is a very empowered thing to do.

Similarly, I have always believed psychic self-defense is extremely important because it is part of being an empowered individual who lives in not only a physical world, but a spiritual one as well. Even though we are living in the physical realm right now, there are energies and entities all around us. Our world is multi-dimensional. There are many things around us that the majority of people cannot see with their physical eyesight, but those energies still have an impact on us.

This is why I have always taught my students about healthy energy boundaries and psychic protection.

While I had always interwoven concepts of psychic

self-defense into my class curriculum, the topic had not been a primary focus for my work, that is, not until the spring of 2016. A very terrifying, profound, and powerful experience catapulted me into a higher calling. In some ways, it has been a more difficult calling, but very rewarding, nonetheless. This has involved focusing more fully on work with psychic self-defense. My work began to include assisting people who are being harassed and attacked by entities and dark energies, people who are experiencing psychic attack from human beings, and so on. What I went through in the spring of 2016 pushed me way beyond my comfort zone, in every way possible. I do not ever wish to go through that experience again, and yet I know deep in my bones that having that experience was vital to putting me on my current path.

So, what happened in the spring of 2016? This book details the entire story, as well as all the valuable knowledge I gained along the way. In short, I experienced an intense, terrifying, powerful, and mind-boggling psychic attack that included black magick, psychological manipulation, sexual violation, and attacks by dark entities including demons. The story is indeed 'stranger than fiction,' and I truly could not have made this stuff up, even if I had tried.

This attack occurred because I came into contact with some colleagues in my spiritual community who were secretly working with Dark Forces. In short, I was able to see the truth of what was really happening, and because I could see past the illusion, I became a primary target. It remains to be seen whether these individuals are fully aware of being influenced by the dark. My heart is open, and I send them prayers, love, and understanding. I always try to remain humble as I remind myself daily, "There but for the grace of God, go I." Perhaps in a different timeline, it could have been me in their shoes being controlled, oppressed, and manipulated by the dark powers that be, and I thank God that is not the case.

This book is not at all about calling out any particular individuals or disparaging anyone's reputation. That is simply not how I roll. For this reason, the names, locations, and identifying information of all of the individuals in the story have been changed. My observation has been that these types of issues occur to some extent in nearly all spiritual communities. The Dark Forces have had a very long history of trying to infiltrate the light by hiding in plain sight within spiritual and personal development populations. My goal is to bring these issues out into the open so that you, the reader, can have a greater awareness of what is out there and make more informed choices as you navigate through the world.

Over the years of teaching and working in spiritual circles, I have observed an overall lack of discernment when people are channeling entities, angels, and spirit guides. In many cases during channeling, there are beings that come through that are not of the Light, that are not of God. These beings are, in fact, imposters; they are the dark disguised as light. Overly trusting practitioners open themselves up to receive messages, assuming they are working with an angel or ascended guide, not even guessing that what they have called in is not what it presents itself to be. The deceiving entity will attach itself to the practitioner. It then absorbs life force energy off of all of that practitioner's clients. This is not an uncommon occurrence. In fact, it is shockingly prevalent.

Interestingly, I have encountered a large number of people in the New Age community who believe that evil does not exist, that malevolent forces do not exist, that dark entities do not exist, that only love and light exist and all else is illusion. Nearly every day in my Facebook newsfeed, I see memes that say, "The light, the dark, there is no difference," emphasizing the common spiritual teaching of oneness, non-polarity, and the acceptance of all. The individuals I've encountered who *do* believe in dark energies have often expressed a belief that evil entities are simply not capable of harming human beings. On the contrary, those who have actually had malevolent spiritual experiences firsthand know and believe the truth. Psychic attacks and dark entities do exist, and they can cause real and significant harm.

The psychic attack I experienced in the spring of 2016 was by far the most terrifying and jarring experience of my life. From start to finish, the entire course of the attack lasted about six weeks, but it felt like an eternity. It started off as a somewhat mild psychological psychic attack but then escalated into a full-out attack by entities, including very evil demonic beings. The attacks became so powerful and malevolent that I truly feared for my life. I have always considered myself to be a pretty brave person when it comes to spiritual matters. After all, I have seen ghosts my whole life. I am definitely not a scaredy-cat, but this situation truly scared the crap out of me!

What was even more disturbing, upsetting, and unsettling was that when I reached out to people for much-needed support and advice, there were very few who understood what I was talking about. Quite simply, they had never experienced a psychic attack or an encounter with a malevolent being (which, by the way, I think is a huge blessing for them). Very few people could relate to what I was going through, which led to me feeling quite alone in the midst of a very traumatic event. Most who had never had this type of personal experience would tell me that I was making the story up, that they don't believe in such things, that what I was going through was literally impossible and complete rubbish.

Another aspect of non-support showed up in the guise of love and light spiritual teachings. Nowadays, there is a very popular spiritual belief that if you just surround yourself in love and light, nothing dark can ever touch you. There is also a common teaching that you will attract to you things that are aligned with your current energy vibration, so if something negative happens to you (like a car accident or illness), it is because you were radiating at that lower vibration. Numerous times, I was told by well-meaning spiritual seekers that I had literally caused these attacks because of some darkness within myself. I remember one person saying, "There must have been something in your vibration that drew this to you." It was pure victim blaming at its finest.

While it is indeed true that we often attract similar vibrations to ourselves, what's equally true is that opposites attract. Let me be crystal clear. When you have a very strong inner light, it can actually make you a target of the Dark Forces. There are hundreds, if not thousands, of accounts throughout recorded history of saints and devout individuals being prime targets of demonic attack. There's a common teaching that radiating love and light will protect you from all darkness. This popular belief is not only false, but it is also dangerous and misleading. I don't share this to initiate fear, but rather, to help spread truth. When you know what makes you vulnerable, you can take practical steps for your own protection and empowerment.

In addition to the lack of moral support from my community, there was also a serious lack of knowledge. I was seeking out spiritual teachers, healers, and anyone who would know how to handle advanced psychic attacks. The really common practices of burning sage, calling in angels, and visualizing white light were not working at all in this situation. This attack was so extreme and so powerful that none of those soft techniques were effective at all, not one bit. I reached out to numerous people, saying, "None of that stuff is working. What do I do for the really extreme stuff?" Nobody had a clue. I kept thinking, "Surely other people have gone through experiences like this. How is it that no one knows what to do?" I even tried contacting two priests in the Catholic Church, and they did not believe what I was telling them. After several weeks of living through hell, I finally connected with a couple of people who had some nuggets of wisdom to share. Aside from that, I had very little support in figuring out how to get through this very treacherous situation.

I was desperate to find answers, and there were very few people who had any information to help. I remember going online and doing research to try to find a community or some people who knew how to deal with severe entity attacks. I could not find anything. There were virtually no resources online. I remember thinking, "Why is there not a support group for this???" I knew in my heart that there were other people with similar experiences, and that those people were also struggling through it on their own. At that moment, I made a deep and sincere vow that once I got through this, I would help others by sharing my knowledge. I can't imagine anybody else having to feel the way that I felt, feeling alone, feeling the lack of support, and being terrified for my life and for the safety of my soul, having no support whatsoever. I don't want anyone else to ever have to feel that way, to experience such a horrible thing without support. That was the reason why I started doing the work that I'm doing now — teaching and assisting people with issues of psychic protection.

There was apparently no credible information available regarding how to clear severe spiritual attacks. I found very few people who knew anything more than just the basics. I did have a couple of teachers that I connected with, and I am eternally grateful for them. With the information from those teachers, and some other earth angels who gave me tips along the way, I was able to completely clear out all of the effects of the psychic attacks, showing me firsthand that the techniques I found were not only useful, but extremely effective. Eventually, I was able to get back to my usual peaceful life, for which I am so very grateful! There were times during the attacks when I believed that those entities were going to be after me for the rest of my life. I was afraid that I would never be able to clear them.

Luckily, the techniques I found are super powerful, effective, and not very difficult to complete. I have been helping to spread this knowledge. What I recognize is that, apparently, I know a lot more about psychic protection than most people, and yet there is still so much more to learn. Every day, I am researching, reading books, studying, going online, consulting with teachers, doing my own spiritual practices, and also connecting with my own spiritual team—my spirit guides and angels—through meditation, as I bring in new information about what is going on in the spiritual realm and which techniques are most effective for resolving various types of psychic protection issues.

Going through this experience was like walking through fire. It was the most uncomfortable, frightening, and painful experience of my life, and yet it strengthened me in ways I cannot even describe. My spirit is so much stronger and braver than I ever thought possible. I feel very blessed to now be sharing this knowledge with the world. I believe that every person on the planet would benefit from learning about psychic protection—what makes you vulnerable, how to identify a psychic attack, what types of energies can harm you, and how to protect yourself and your loved ones.

The good news is that most people will never have issues with extreme psychic attack, but a fraction of the population will. Those who work in the field of spirituality are often prime targets, and this includes spiritual teachers, clergy, energy healers, psychics, mediums, etc. On the other hand, anyone can become a target, because sometimes it can simply be a matter of being in the wrong place at the wrong time. Whether a person experiences mild or severe issues regarding psychic attack, *everyone* needs information, support, protection, and empowerment about this important topic.

ABOUT THE BOOK

With each chapter of this book, my personal stories about psychic attack unfold, and along with these stories, I include the lessons I have learned along the way. The beginning of the book focuses on relevant stories from my childhood and early adulthood that set the stage for the primary story in this book, while the later chapters retell the fascinating story of one single complex psychic attack that occurred in the spring of 2016. At the end of each chapter, I have included core lessons and exercises that you can apply to your own life.

The stories and lessons build from chapter to chapter, starting with somewhat basic training and moving into material relating to more complicated and powerful psychic attacks. In addition, the main story itself is a multi-layered mystery that unfolds from chapter to chapter. Because of this, it is best to read this book from start to finish, taking in each lesson as you go, and pondering each level of the story. After the first reading, you may choose to use this book as a reference tool, flipping to the training at the end of each chapter as needed.

On a side note, I would like to clarify that even though some of my experiences include aspects from specific religious traditions, this book in no way promotes any one spiritual or religious practice over another. While my childhood upbringing included strong notes of Catholic and Christian mysticism, my current spiritual beliefs encompass a broad range of faiths, including Buddhist, Native American, neo-Pagan, New Age, and more, including beliefs that do not fit into any particular box whatsoever.

Whether you currently follow a particular religion or spiritual path or were exposed to a particular path in your younger years, I believe that your past and present beliefs can play a part in your experiences around psychic protection. Your current and past belief systems, whatever they may be, can be a huge source of comfort and extremely powerful protection for you. Even if you no longer actively practice or believe in the particular faith of your upbringing, I believe there is imprinting that occurs on a subconscious level, so that when you are in need of serious spiritual protection, the practices and beliefs of your childhood can hold tremendous power.

My hope is that every person reading this book will receive the knowledge and tools they need to create a safe and empowered life for themselves and their loved ones. Whether you are simply curious about psychic protection, or you have experienced a mild to extreme psychic attack, I believe you will find practical information to keep you safe, protected, and powerful.

CHAPTER 1 – EARLY SPIRITUAL BEGINNINGS

Ever since I can remember, I have had a connection with the world of spirit. Earlier in life, most of my experiences were positive and uplifting and revolved around the Divine, angels, and the higher aspects of the spirit world. Equally as memorable were the few experiences that did involve negative and frightening situations.

As an infant, I was adopted into a conservative Irish Catholic family and I became the youngest of five children. Although my family went to church and were devout about following Catholic doctrine, they were not particularly spiritual. I, on the other hand, had numerous mystical experiences starting from early childhood. When I was a toddler, I remember one particular priest whom I knew was different from the others because I always saw a golden glow of light emanating around his head during Mass. As a child, I could also feel energy flowing through my body and I could sense the emotions of those around me.

Even though my family was not particularly spiritual, I always had a special connection with the spiritual even from a young age. When I was four years old, I was sitting in the church pew next to my mother when I suddenly had a very vivid flashback from a time before I was born. I was in a black void that seemed like space but with no stars. I looked at myself and, instead of having a body, I was beautiful pure light energy. In that flashback, I remembered meeting with other light beings and making plans for my upcoming life. One of the beings was my mother. We were making an agreement to work together in this lifetime and she was going to adopt me and become my mother. In the flashback, I knew that I was an older, wiser spirit than her, and that even though I was to be her child, she would be the one learning many things from me in this lifetime.

When I came out of this flashback, I asked my mother, "Mommy, did I know you before I was born?" "I don't know, I suppose so," she said, patting me on the head, not realizing the importance of my question. Despite having a difficult relationship with her throughout my life, I always remembered that childhood vision. I always believed that our relationship had purpose and had been mutually chosen.

As a pre-teen, I was out bike riding with one of my best friends. We were riding around a shopping center parking lot where there happened to also be a mortuary. We rode our bikes behind the mortuary toward our route back home, and as she pedaled ahead of me, I suddenly got a very strong chill down the back of my neck. I stopped my bike and looked toward the building. Standing there on the back stoop, I saw an old man. He appeared transparent and was looking with puzzlement from side to side, as though he was wondering where he was. My friend suddenly started calling me because she had ridden way ahead. I caught up with her and told her what I had seen, but she did not believe me.

As a teenager, the spiritual experiences increased exponentially. I began having experiences with precognitive dreams (dreaming about events before they actually happened), telepathy with friends, clairvoyance (visions), and clairaudience (auditory messages). On numerous occasions I had visions of Jesus, Mother Mary, angels, and on a few occasions, I also had encounters with dark beings. I was a very spiritually devout teenager — pretty unusual for someone at that age.

The encounters with dark beings were few and far between compared to the many encounters I had with the light, with beings that were from God. I had daily connection with the divine, which included deep prayer, powerful visions, dreams, and spiritual encounters on a regular basis, and as a deeply spiritual teenager, having mystical experiences became quite normal for me.

Once when I was at a gathering with my high school church youth group, I had a powerful experience that was validated by many other members of the group. We had just gathered into a circle for the opening prayer. Right at the moment when we all took hands, I saw a flash of white light in the center of the circle and I felt a powerful energy that quickly surged around the circle from one person to the next through our joined hands. I was accustomed to experiencing a lot of unusual spiritual things in my daily life, more than what most people seem to experience, so I just assumed that I was the only one who had sensed the powerful energy. To my surprise, after the twenty-minute prayer was complete, everyone immediately started to comment on the energy surge they had felt.

I was amazed and excited to receive validation that others had felt what I had. Even when I have experienced something firsthand, I do not automatically believe in it, and because of this, I have always been happy when other people pick up on the same things I do. I jokingly call myself an "open-minded skeptic." I am open to many different possibilities, but I do not automatically believe in something without a certain amount of questioning and scrutiny.

On another occasion, I had a profound vision that was so amazing I hesitated to tell anyone about it at first. I remember that it was late on a mild Friday afternoon after I had gotten home from school. Every Friday I was required to do the household chores assigned to me. My dad was not home from work yet and my mom was in a really bad mood. I was preparing to scrub the entryway floor, and so I picked up the entry rug to go shake it outside. My mom said something harsh to me, and I remember feeling discouraged and sad. I picked up the rug and walked out the front door. On the front stoop, I turned to the right to shake the rug. A tremendous gust of wind suddenly blew so hard that it rocked me back on my heels. I was suddenly transported to a place that was timeless. There was a beautiful bright golden light in front of me and Jesus was standing in the middle of the light. I remember that he was slightly shorter than me and his skin looked like golden light was emanating from it. He reached out his hand and touched my cheek as though he was making a gesture of comfort. I stood there with no sense of time passing and I remember that I had absolutely no thoughts in my mind except for one..."This is so beautiful." Standing there, I was filled with a level of peace beyond anything I had ever experienced before.

The next thing I knew, I was walking back into the front door of my house. As I stood there in the front hallway, I gasped and thought, "Wait a minute, what just happened?" With my normal scrutiny, I considered how I had been distracted by worry and discontent about my mom, that I had not been praying or even thinking about spiritual things when this vision had occurred. I was amazed at what had happened. After I finished my chores, I called the church youth group assistant leader, Jackie, and told her what happened. I stammered and had a hard time getting it out. I felt that it was so unbelievable she would think I was making it up. But with her gentle encouragement, I finally told her. I will never forget her response. "I'm not surprised at all that this happened to you." I was puzzled. "What do you mean?" I asked. "What I mean is that you have such a deep devotion to God, this type of thing was bound to happen to you sooner or later."

The White Moth
Even as a teen, I began to understand the idea that those who have a very bright light can sometimes be targeted by the dark powers. When I was sixteen years old, I was hanging out in our finished basement with

my high school boyfriend, Sam, when I suddenly got a very dark foreboding sense of an evil energy across the room from us. By that time, I was quite used to having paranormal experiences, but I had had very few of an evil nature. Not sure if what I was feeling was really accurate, I did not say anything to my boyfriend, but rather, I continued to listen to him chat about his day. Suddenly, he stopped talking mid-sentence. Sam looked at me, pale-faced, and said, "I was trying to ignore it, but I just have this horrible feeling that there's something evil here with us. Do you feel it?" I was shocked. "Yes," I said in a low voice. "I felt it but didn't say anything." Wanting to validate if what I had been feeling was accurate, I asked him to point out where in the room he was feeling this presence. I refrained from telling him where I was feeling it. He stood up, walked across the room and pointed at a specific place on the floor. "Oh my God," I exclaimed. "That's exactly where I feel it, too." "Look," he said, "There's a dead white moth on the floor exactly where we're feeling that presence." "That's weird," I responded. We sat there for a few moments more and then we mutually decided to go back upstairs to hang out in the living room instead.

The next morning, I woke before the rest of the family. Sleepy and bleary-eyed I walked toward the kitchen in the dim light. Suddenly, I got a huge chill down my neck and felt a very evil presence standing between me and the kitchen doorway. Knowing that my parents would not believe me, and not having any knowledge yet how to clear out such energies, I cautiously walked over and turned on the kitchen lights. To my surprise, I saw a dead white moth on the floor in the exact spot where I had felt the evil presence. Of course, I called my boyfriend and told him all about it, but to this day, we still do not know what it all meant.

Deliver Us from Evil
A few months later I woke early in the morning to the sound of rock music playing on my clock radio. In my half-awake state, I heard the words, "Satan is my savior." Assuming that it was part of the lyrics of the song, I rolled onto my side and opened my eyes. To my surprise, I saw a young man, about my age, standing at the side of my bed as though he was watching over me. He was average weight and height, had short brown hair, had a very pale complexion, and was wearing a long black robe with a hood over his head. Thinking I must be imagining things, I closed my eyes, rubbed them a few times, and then reopened them. The young man was gone. For the next few days, I tried to figure out what song I had awoken to so I could scrutinize the lyrics, but unfortunately, the song remained a mystery.

I spoke with Jackie about it. She was concerned, but she also told me she was not surprised. She said that because I was such an unusually devout young woman, I was a threat to the Dark Forces. She encouraged me to pray for protection and safety. I did not tell my parents about the situation because I did not feel they would understand or believe me. For the next few days, I was quite nervous and jumpy that something evil or scary would appear to me again, and I had quite a bit of trouble sleeping. Since I had an active relationship with Mother Mary at the time, I began wearing a rosary around my neck while sleeping for extra protection and comfort. After a few more days without any frightening activity, I began to relax and resume my usual daily routine.

Calling Mother Mary

About a year later, I had another scary encounter. I had just returned home from working an evening shift at the frozen yogurt shop. It was late and my parents were already in bed. I walked upstairs to my bedroom and I suddenly felt a very evil presence in the hallway. I did not see anything, but I could feel the presence very strongly. I had no doubt about what I was feeling, so I immediately called on Mother Mary for protection. I felt her presence appear and I knew that she reached out her hand in comfort to touch me on the arm. Her touch felt cool on my arm. I looked down and carefully inspected my forearm where she had touched me and saw that I had goosebumps. So, then I inspected both arms, and validated that I *only* had goosebumps on the section of the one arm where she had touched me, and nowhere else.

I was exhausted from work, so I put my rosary around my neck, said some fervent prayers for protection, and crawled under the covers. As I drifted off to sleep, I saw a vision of Mary's face looking over me and I felt her cool hand touch my forehead. In hindsight, I am surprised I fell asleep almost instantly. It was as though I had taken a powerful sleeping pill. Several times during the night, I would begin to wake up, yet something kept me from waking up all the way. I had the sense that major spiritual warfare was occurring in the room and that Mary was kicking some serious butt as this dark being was trying to get to me. When I woke in the morning, I recalled what I had sensed during the night. I believed that my protector, Mary, had been keeping me asleep through it all so that I would not be afraid. I noticed that I felt completely peaceful and that my bedroom now felt light and airy, totally free of any negative energy.

Finding My Way in The World
As a young adult during and after college, I went through a period of spiritual crisis as I tried to make sense of my faith. Growing up, I had always questioned every aspect of what I had been taught to believe in the Catholic and Christian churches I had attended. I chuckle when I think of how exasperated my father would become when I would ask him about church teachings. Every time I would ask questions, he would snap, "You're not supposed to question it. You're supposed to just believe!" But my questioning would always persist, whether it was with my father, the priests, or the youth group leaders.

When I moved away from home to attend college and start work, the questioning increased even more. I was working as a teacher at the local Catholic schools and, although I loved the faith of my upbringing, it felt like there were other truths out there as well. Eventually, I left the Catholic Church and began exploring a more eclectic spiritual path that still includes the mysticism of the Catholic Church, plus many diverse teachings from a variety of traditions.

In 1997 (in my mid-20s) I began experiencing a huge personal and spiritual transformation. I ended a controlling abusive relationship I had been in for three years. As I began to reclaim my personal power and my life purpose, I started studying energy healing, Reiki, intuitive development, and even sacred movement and belly dance. I had previously abandoned my purpose and my personal power in order to stay in the mainstream box, as well as keep the peace in my relationship. Once I kicked through the wall of mainstream existence, I never looked back.

The Dancing Angel
The day I left my partner was one of the hardest days of my life. Yet it led to a very beautiful and touching spiritual experience that confirmed for me that I was on the right path. My parents had come into town to help me pack up and move out. Suspecting that something was happening, my ex-boyfriend had come home early from work to discover that I was leaving. He was a very controlling, manipulative, and emotionally abusive person, and with the blessing of my parish priest and my family, I was trying to escape that horrible situation.

My parents and I finally got everything packed and moved out. It had been an extremely stressful and exhausting day. My head was spinning. As a master manipulator, my former partner was an expert at berating me to the point of mental confusion, making me feel like my brain had been put in a blender. Because of this, I was questioning whether I was making a huge mistake by leaving. In hindsight, I came to understand this was because I had been systematically brainwashed to believe whatever he told me.

That night, my parents and I stayed at a local hotel. My mom and I slept in one of the queen beds, and my dad took the other bed. I fell into an exhausted and strange sleep. It felt as though all night long, for hours and hours, I was having the same dream. I was an angel with beautiful white wings and luminous white light emanating from me. I was standing in the middle of a wind-blown meadow, and I was spinning around and around in circles, dancing with my arms outstretched up, laughing and laughing with so much joy because I was finally free.

When I woke up, my mom was already in the bathroom brushing her hair. "Mom," I said, "I think I made the right decision. I just had the most amazing dream." I told her about how I had dreamt I was an angel and how I had been dancing and spinning and laughing with joy. She said, "Well, you were laughing out loud all night long!" "I was?!" I asked incredulously. "Really? All night long?" "Yes, really," she said as she began putting on her make-up. "Wow," I mumbled to myself, as I pondered the importance of the dream. I knew I had made the right choice. My spirit was showing me that I was now free and on the right path.

For the next month, I stayed with a friend until I found a place of my own. It was New Year's Eve 1998 when I moved into my new rental house. I was unpacking boxes and feeling a little down that I was spending New Year's Eve all alone. As I was unpacking, I brought some items into my bedroom, and to my surprise, when I walked through the door, I saw an angel with huge white wings hovering horizontally over my little twin bed. I was immediately filled with comfort and peace about my situation, and I knew that I was being watched over and protected.

Black Magick Hex
About six years later I experienced my first personal psychic attack, sent to me deliberately by someone practicing black magick. Previous to this, I could not believe that someone would use energy to maliciously harm another person. To my knowledge, I had never experienced an intentional psychic attack, so I was in completely new territory. At that time, I was self-employed working with my energy healing clients and students, and on the side, I was also teaching belly dancing classes to women at the local parks and recreation departments throughout New Orleans.

One of the dance students approached me after class one night and asked if she could redo my website for me at a reduced price. She explained that she was a website designer, that she could tell my simple website was self-made, and that she really wanted to help me have a more professional, polished website. I explained that I was on a shoestring budget, so she graciously offered a special reduced price, saying that she was really enjoying my classes and she wanted to help me out. And so, she moved forward with the website and I began to make payments for her work.

Once the site was complete, I had some ongoing changes that needed to be made, including regular updates to the dance class schedules. At first, she was available to make these changes and all seemed fine. But then, within a couple of weeks she suddenly went MIA. The class schedules were out of date and she was not responding to my messages. After a couple of weeks of trying to contact her, I left another message asking her to please get back to me. I could sense that she was upset and not talking to me, but I did not know why. I felt like my unfinished website was being held hostage.

Finally, one day I got an email from a concerned student. "Maya, did you know that your website has been removed?" "What?!" I panicked as I scrambled to pull up my website. I typed in the URL. My website was gone, and in its place was a black page with a cryptic message with misspellings stating that the website was no longer available.

I checked my email again and found an email from the student who had created my website. The email was many pages long, explaining how angry she was with me, how she felt that I had not paid her enough for her work, and that if I wanted the website back, I would have to pay her several thousand dollars. I was panicked. I did not have that kind of money. My business and my income depended on my website so people could find my classes and pay for them online. What was I going to do? I was so shocked by what this student had done! I called her and left a voicemail, begging her to please put my website back online, but she did not return my call.

That night, I was fast asleep when I suddenly woke up and bolted upright in my bed. With my psychic vision, I could see this student standing at the foot of my bed. I looked at my clock and it was midnight. I knew from prior conversations with this student that she was a practicing witch. Was she doing some sort of spell work on me? I have many friends from a variety of spiritual paths, but at the time, I had never considered that someone would use their spiritual knowledge to cause harm. I had a feeling of foreboding as I felt goosebumps all over my body and my hair stand on end. I was concerned but did not know what could be done except to go back to sleep. I tried to put it all out of my mind.

The next morning, I awoke to a terrible stench in my apartment. My boyfriend noticed it, too, but even after looking everywhere, we could not find the origin of the horrible smell. My downstairs neighbors came knocking at the door, complaining about the odor. We all agreed to call the landlord who came out to check the property. Nothing was found.

Over the next three days, I noticed an inordinate number of issues with our electronics and vehicles. My computer, my boyfriend's, and my assistant's all crashed. My car stalled, and my boyfriend's and assistant's cars all broke down. My assistant only lived three blocks away and was driving to my house to meet me for a business meeting. She commented on how unusual it was that her car broke down because it had never had problems before. The next day, I went to the home of the new web designer I had hired, and she mentioned that she had barely gotten home in time to meet with me since her car had unexpectedly broken down.

When I became aware of yet another car breaking down, I finally realized that I had been in denial and I had a real problem on my hands. When I got home, I psychically tuned into the energy of my apartment, and I perceived an angry bright red mist through every room and even outside on the front porch. I then admitted to myself that I was dealing with a real psychic attack and I needed to do something about it. I was afraid and on guard for a few days, feeling like I was at the mercy of this very unbalanced individual and her black magick.

After a few days, I came to a sense of clarity. I realized that she was acting like a bully and that bullies are activated by the fear and helplessness of their victims. Suddenly, I felt an inner power within me well up. I knew that she was powerless to harm me if I was not afraid of her. I imagined how I would respond if I was having an encounter with a bully face to face. I would stand up with a flippant demeanor and say, "Whatever, babe. I'm not giving you any of my attention," then I would laugh and turn the other way. Energetically, that's what I did.

In the following days, whenever I felt any energies of the psychic attack, instead of falling into fear, I would just say, "Whatever, you don't deserve my attention!" The psychic attack quickly dissipated and I had no more issues after that. I can only assume that she was only a novice at black magick. While she was indeed able to initiate a psychic attack directed toward me, it was extremely easy to clear the attack with very little effort. Had she been a master magician, it is likely that the attack would have been much more challenging to clear.

LESSON 1 – WHAT IS A PSYCHIC ATTACK?

Psychic attacks are more common than you might imagine, and they range from barely noticeable to full out life-threatening spiritual warfare. Every day, we are affected by unseen energies that can have either positive or negative influence in our lives.

The most common attacks are sent unintentionally. UNINTENTIONAL psychic attacks occur when a person unconsciously sends negative energy your way. The person may be experiencing negative thoughts, intentions, or emotions relating to you, or having feelings of anger, resentment, jealousy or even hatred toward you. Regardless of whether the person is aware they are sending a psychic attack, intense emotion-filled thoughts directed toward another person will indeed have a negative impact. Even if the upset person has buried their feelings deep in their subconscious mind and they are not even consciously aware of how they feel, the negative energy still seeps out. Unintentional psychic attacks can affect your energy like little daggers cutting tiny holes in your aura. Over time, these holes develop into larger areas of damage which cause your overall energy field to weaken. This, in turn, can cause depression, anxiety, decrease of vitality and well-being, and even make you more vulnerable to more serious psychic attacks.

Focused negative intent (unintentional or intentional) can also cause energy cords to attach from the perpetrator to the recipient. We will cover energy cords in depth in chapter 3.

In addition, when someone focuses strongly on a particular thought or feeling, it can create an energetic phenomenon called a 'thought form.' The person's focused intent literally brings an energetic entity into being. These phenomena can be created unintentionally by people who are sending out their unconscious negative emotions. This energetic thought form, which now has a consciousness all its own, can directly assault the victim. This form of psychic attack can take on the characteristics of an entity attack because the thought form acts very much like a dark being. Additionally, other thought forms can be created quite purposefully by magickal practitioners who are casting intentional spells to bring an entity into reality to attack someone.

Locations can also be a source of unintentional psychic attack. Chronically dysfunctional environments filled with conflict, stress, unhappiness, and drama can carry negative vibrations that can be detrimental to your own energy field. Negative locations can include a workplace, home, or any other place where there is a high level of chronic stress. Some locations can even carry residual negative energies from past traumas that took place there, like abuse, murder, suicide, famine, genocide, etc. Battlefields, concentration camps, and even hospitals can hold a great deal of dark, depressive energy due to the tremendous amount of suffering and large number of deaths that have occurred there. Living, working, or even visiting any of these environments can be quite taxing to the average person's energy.

INTENTIONAL psychic attacks are sent with conscious, malevolent intent by either a person or an evil spirit. Unfortunately, there are human beings on our planet who believe it is acceptable to send a curse, hex, or black magick. Those who direct purposeful harm toward others have the twisted belief that they are entitled to do so in order to achieve their personal goals. There are so many spiritual paths available in our world, and some people choose to utilize the shadow aspects of these paths. From my own observation, most of us do not want to believe that people would do such things. One important truth to keep in mind is that just because YOU would never dream of doing such things does not mean that others have the same integrity you do. Black magick, hexes, and curses actually do occur, and there are those who use these dark methods without remorse or hesitation. Having this understanding will put you one step ahead with your awareness and personal safety.

Non-physical beings (spirits, demons, etc.) can also send intentional psychic attacks. In the physical human world, individuals are typically neither all good nor all bad, but rather, they are a complex mixture of both. The same is true (for the most part) in the spiritual realm. Earthbound spirits, for example, are human beings who have died and passed on to the etheric realm, and just like humans, they have complex personalities that are neither all good nor all bad. These earthbound spirits are souls who avoid moving on to the other side (what some think of as Heaven) due to unfinished business, over-attachment to worldly desires (like alcohol, drugs, sex, or other addictions), or fear, internal conflict, or disbelief relating to the afterlife. While many of these discarnate souls are benign and completely harmless, others are operating from a very low vibration in which their main goal is to cause harm.

Some beings in the spiritual realm have consciously and willingly chosen to polarize completely on the side of darkness and evil. Demons and other dark entities deliberately work to initiate fear and suffering on the planet.

AN IMPORTANT SIDE NOTE...
As soon as I finished typing the previous sentence, a transformer suddenly blew in my neighborhood and the electricity went out not only in my home, but through the whole block. I immediately recognized the negative synchronicity that was occurring. It was no random coincidence that the lights had inexplicably gone out as soon as I started writing about how the Dark Forces strive to manipulate people through fear. I am quite aware that the dark powers do not want me to write this book and reveal the truth, and they will do things like this to make me too afraid to continue my project. Thankfully, their fear tactics no longer work on me like they once did.

I stood up and slowly scuffled through my pitch black kitchen, hands feeling in front of me for the shelf that held my emergency flashlight. I spoke some prayers aloud as I turned on the flashlight and then lit some candles. I was nervous and aware, but not terrified. There have been numerous odd experiences that have occurred when I have tried to write, speak, or make audios or videos about this content. This time,

I knew I should remain alert but not allow the situation to pull me into fear. From my past experiences, I knew all too well that the blackout was just a stunt to stir me up and make me too afraid to continue with this book. Most of the tactics are smoke and mirrors, and I don't fall for them anymore.

Yet, I could definitely feel a very dark energy in the house with me. I took immediate empowered action by sending messages to two different groups of friends, telling them what was going on and asking them to collectively send light to my home. I also grabbed my phone and immediately started streaming a live video on my Psychic Protection Sanctuary Facebook group as I talked about what was happening. There is strength in numbers, and the more people that send light, prayers, and positive intent, the more powerful the positive impact. Plus, I did not want to go through the experience alone.

My phone was about to die, so I finished the live video, then sat in the candlelight for a moment. As I tuned into the dark presence that was there with me, I could feel that it was quite annoyed with me. Its scheme had not worked. Suddenly, all the lights in the house came back on. The entity was gone. Not only were the house lights back on, but the house also seemed as though it was filled with a beautiful bright spiritual light. I tuned into the environment and could feel the presence of angels. I knew that I was safe and that the minor attack had passed without much incident.

MORE ABOUT INTENTIONAL ATTACKS

As I was saying before my writing was interrupted, demons and other dark entities deliberately work to initiate fear and suffering on the planet. The goal of these dark beings is to manipulate and source energy from human beings. Here is how it works: The evil entity attaches to the aura of a person, most often someone who is in a vulnerable state, like depression, past trauma, addictions, etc. The dark being works to stir up even more of the depression, trauma, addiction, or even violent tendencies by sending the person negative thoughts and urges. The entity then feeds off of the suffering of the individual.

Similarly, the evil spirit will also choose to attack a person whose light is seen as a threat to the dark. The purpose is to keep the lightworker weak so they are unable to complete their positive life purpose. This can be done in the way described above, by initiating depression, trauma, and addiction. Alternately, the malevolent goal can be obtained by sending demonically possessed people into the person's life, especially in the role of romantic partner whose position is to abuse, oppress, and source energy off of the individual. Another avenue is through outright entity attack where the person is literally tormented by the dark energy being through dreams, waking apparitions, and even physical or sexual assault.

Some of this might seem a bit outlandish, but I assure you, it is absolutely true. Over the years, I have worked with countless clients who are healing from such circumstances, and I have also experienced these things firsthand in my own life. Psychic attacks really do range from mild and barely noticeable to exceedingly terrifying and life threatening. Every person in the world has experienced at least mild psychic attacks due to simply being alive and going through life's ups and downs and stresses. Now is the time to take stock of where your issues fall on the spectrum from mild to severe.

EXERCISE

Personal Evaluation

In your journal or notebook, answer the questions below. Completing this exercise will help you gain clarity on whether you may have possible vulnerabilities to psychic attack or entity attack. Remain open to any areas of your life where you might need to bring more attention to your personal psychic protection.

The questions cover a broad range of topics, so be sure to go through the whole list. There are thirty questions, so don't spend too much time on any one question. Set your timer for ten minutes and go through them quickly and in a focused manner. You can always go back at a later time and spend more time journaling and going through past memories. Our goal now is to simply identify any areas that may make you more vulnerable to spiritual attack.

Do not be worried or afraid if you answer 'yes' to any of the questions below. Knowledge is power. Once you learn what makes you more vulnerable, you can continue reading the book to uncover numerous valuable tools to aid in your safety and security, no matter your history or vulnerabilities.

This exercise is to help you gain personal clarity as it applies to the concepts in this book; however, it is not a replacement for therapy or medical treatment. Please consult your medical practitioner or therapist for any support you may need.

1. Have you ever experienced any type of abuse at any time in your past? This could include physical, verbal, emotional, psychological, sexual, or other. The abuse could have occurred within your family, with a romantic partner or spouse, from a friend or acquaintance, in the workplace, or other.

Remember, it is not necessary to go deep into these memories (unless you wish to do so). For now, your goal is to simply identify when, with whom, and how the abuse occurred, as well as a sentence or two about how it has continued to impact you in your life. Write your answers in your notebook or journal.

2. Have you ever been sexually assaulted? Again, it is not necessary to go deeply into these memories, but rather, to simply identify that it happened, when, and what was going on in your life at the time. Record your answers.

3. Do you have a history of mental health issues including depression or anxiety? If so, can you identify when these issues originally began? What was going on in your life at the time? Can you identify a trigger that brings on the depression or anxiety?

4. Do you have a history of serious psychiatric issues? If so, when did the issues originally begin? Have you sought medical treatment?

5. Have you ever attempted suicide? Yes or no, and

what was going on in your life at the time?

6. Have you experienced any sort of personal trauma or loss, including the death of someone close to you; losing your home to fire, flood, or natural disaster; losing your job or business; bankruptcy; or other? When and how did it occur?

7. Have you ever been the victim of a crime? If so, what was the crime, when did it occur, who was involved, and what was going on in your life at the time?

8. Have you been in a minor or major auto accident? When and how did it occur? What was going on in your life at the time? What were your injuries? Did you receive medical treatment?

9. Have you ever committed a crime? If so, when, what did you do, and why?

10. Have you ever been convicted and incarcerated for a crime? When, for how long, where, and why? Record your answers.

11. Have you experienced chronic or acute illness? What, when, and for how long? What was going on in your life at the onset of the illness?

12. Have you had a major surgery or major medical procedure in the past? If so, when was it and what was it for? Were you under anesthesia for the procedure?

13. Do you use recreational drugs, or have you used

them in the past? If so, what did you use, how often, and why?

14. Do you have any type of addiction, including drugs, alcohol, food, sex, gambling, or etc.? If so, when did the problem begin, and what was going on in your life at the time? Have you sought out treatment?

15. Do you have issues with bouts of anger, aggression, or violent outbursts? If so, what seems to be the trigger?

16. Do you have a lot of stress in your home or work environment? Yes or no, and why? How long has it been an issue?

17. Would you say there is a lot of drama in your life right now? Are you a high drama person, or are there other people in your life who are high drama? Explain.

18. Do you have difficulty setting and maintaining boundaries with others? Do you have difficulty saying 'no' or communicating your needs to others?
19. Have you ever lived in a house where there was indication of entity activity, including:

___ lights flashing
___ hearing footsteps, knocking, voices, or other unexplainable sounds
___ objects moving for no explainable reason
___ seeing ghosts
___ unexplainable cold spots
___ feeling like you are not alone or there is someone watching you

20. Have you ever used a Ouija board to communicate with the other side?

21. Have you ever worked with black magick, hexes, or curses, to cause harm to another person, or for your own personal gain? Why and how?

22. Have you intentionally called upon demons or evil spirits to do your bidding? Why and how?

23. To your knowledge, have you ever experienced a psychic attack?

24. Have you ever been attacked (physically, psychologically, sexually, or energetically) by an evil entity, demon, or something unexplainable? If so, explain when and how the attack occurred? What was the final result? Was the attack ever completely cleared?

25. Are you a psychic, medium (see or sense spirits), or a spiritual channel?

26. Are you an energy healer, faith healer, Reiki practitioner, shamanic healer, or other lightworker?

27. Are you extra sensitive to the energies and feelings of those around you?

28. Is your life purpose rooted in spreading light and helping others?

29. Are you deeply spiritual or devout in your love for the Divine?

30. Would you say that your physical self-care needs improvement? For example, do you smoke, eat junk food, avoid exercise, or stay indoors all the time?

Now that you are done going through these questions, it is time for some evaluation. Did you answer 'yes' to one or more of the questions above? If so, that means you may be more vulnerable to psychic attack than you realize.

Let's break it down a bit. First of all, any experience whatsoever that involves trauma or stress to your body, mind, or spirit, will inevitably cause some level of damage to your energy body (aura), thus making your system weaker and more vulnerable to attack. If left unchecked, a person can end up having large tears, holes, or missing areas in their aura, or even lacking any energy boundaries whatsoever. Even seemingly mundane situations like a routine medical procedure or a moderately stressful workplace can cause damage to your energetic shield. And of course, traumas of a more serious nature actually leave an imprint in a person's aura, making them a vibrational match for additional victimization, including spiritual attack.

There are some circumstances that can essentially put an energetic target sign on a person. If an individual has had encounters with dark entities in the past, either due to having been a victim of psychic attack, or due to willingly and knowingly calling in evil spirits, any and all dark beings will have easier access to this person in the future. It is like the person has been 'tagged.' In addition, any person who is 'light polarized' — who has a strong alignment and commitment to work with the divine — is seen as a threat to the dark agenda and may be targeted specifically to keep them from shining their light.

No matter how you answered the above questions, do not worry. Once you are done reading this book, you will be armed with numerous powerful methods to help keep you and your loved ones safe. In the next chapter, we will begin to explore some of the important tools and techniques that everyone should learn for their own protection.

CHAPTER 2 – THE SIGHT

A few years ago, I had several experiences that were very troubling and caused me to question my trust in myself and my surroundings. My insights seemed to be much different than that of my colleagues and community, and I wondered why no one else was seeing what I could see. In hindsight, I now understand that, as my psychic abilities were opening even more, I was perceiving aspects of the spiritual world that many others did not yet understand. It was during this period that I learned to trust myself more—even when I received no validation from others. I learned how to give myself permission to either speak up or walk away from energies that did not feel good to me or to assist in clearing those energies if I was called to do so. This self-trust ended up being my saving grace during the severe psychic attacks that would come later.

I have had an ongoing habit of attending various spiritual events around my community as a way of making new connections and friendships, as well as supporting my colleagues and friends at their events. One such event was a spiritually oriented drum circle held at a local yoga studio. It was my first time attending this particular event. As I walked into the studio with a friend of mine, I gave both the event leader and studio owner a great big hug and sat down in the circle with eager, happy anticipation. Both men and women sat in chairs in a large circle, holding a variety of drums including Middle Eastern doumbeks, African djembes, Native American frame drums, and even claves and rattles. I saw some familiar faces including some of my colleagues — spiritual teachers and healers — as well as some unfamiliar faces, too. As the leader began to chant and drum, the participants joined in, drumming to the steady beat. Some even went to the center of the circle to dance and allow the rhythm to flow through them.

I had attended all sorts of community drum circles over the years and had always enjoyed the healing aspects of drumming — the stress relief, the connection with spirit, the creative flow. But something seemed off at this circle. As I flowed with the rhythm of the drummers and dancers, I became aware of a strange dark energy emerging a few feet to my right. I tried to ignore it, but then all of a sudden, the woman sitting in that vicinity began twitching, shaking, moaning, sobbing, and writhing out of control in her chair. I sat there in shock. Everyone kept drumming as though nothing at all was happening. And yet, it was completely clear to me that this young woman was being possessed by a dark entity. Didn't anyone else notice this? It was clear as day! Why wasn't the leader doing something about it? Couldn't she see what was happening? Why hadn't the drum circle leader cleared the energy of the space before the event? Why hadn't she established energetic protection for the participants?

I had always assumed that event facilitators and studio owners understood the importance of creating safe and sacred space. Maybe my assumption had been wrong. Since I was only a visitor at the event, I felt I was not at liberty to intervene. Instead, I just sat there, shocked and puzzled. I never went back to that event.

A few months later, I received an invitation to attend a women's prayer and meditation circle at a local church. In past services at the church, the congregation seemed very open-minded and welcoming. As I considered attending the event, I thought about how it would be a great way to connect with a lovely group of women on my day off. I invited a friend and we headed over to the join the group.

The circle was being held in a small room adjacent to the church. My friend and I walked in and were greeted by about twenty-five women of various different ages. We sat down to begin, and I suddenly felt very ill. My head was swimming. The room felt very hot and stuffy, and for some reason, I felt so fidgety that I wanted to jump out of my skin. I worried that maybe I looked silly fidgeting and moving around in my seat so much. I tried to breathe and ground, but something in the room was making me feel very uncomfortable. Finally, I allowed myself to tune into the room with my psychic vision. (As a very sensitive empath, I do not keep my psychic channels open 100% of the time, because if I did, I would be overloaded with too much information. At this moment, however, I knew I needed to open my vision to understand more fully what was going on.).

As soon as I tuned in, I saw close to fifty ghosts crammed into the already crowded space. I looked around and saw that they were all women, mostly elderly, and seemingly harmless. Intuitively, I knew they had all been prior members of the church when they had been alive, and they eagerly wanted to be a part of this prayer circle. That is not necessarily a bad thing, in and of itself but even benign ghosts can be problematic. First of all, it is probably best for these souls to move into the light, rather than hanging out on the Earth plane. Secondly, it is not in the best interest of the live people at the circle to be surrounded by a large group of ghosts. Even seemingly harmless spirits can attach to living people, sometimes causing interference and negative issues for the person. And third, for anyone psychically sensitive like I am, being in a room full of ghosts can feel totally intolerable and suffocating.

As I tuned in and pondered what was going on with the energy around me, it felt to me that perhaps that room had *never* been cleared. The ghosts I was seeing had been hanging out in that room for a very long time. How could it be that no one who has used the space over the years has ever done any energy clearing there? How could they not know how important this is? I was blown away by this. Or was there something wrong with *me*? I felt very self-conscious for being the one oddball freak in the room that could see and feel the ghosts.

I continued to sit there wiggling around in my chair, trying not to cause too much of a disruption. Having been a teacher and leader for many years, I have always been very careful not to take charge in other people's groups. It is their group, and they should be in charge of the energy. Not wanting to be rude, and not wanting to ruin the experience for my friend, I stayed until the end of the meeting.

When it was through, my friend and I went into the kitchen for a drink of water as I privately told her what I had observed and experienced. I asked if we could leave as soon as possible. I felt like my skin was crawling, I had brain fog, and I could barely breathe. And yet, as soon as we walked out the door onto the front steps of the building, I suddenly felt like I could breathe again. Within a split second I felt clear, grounded, and right as rain.

As we walked down the street, I commented to her how puzzled I was that the people at the church did not know about the ghosts and how they were not clearing their space on a regular basis. I was a little shaken up and filled with self-doubt. I was confused why the other people had seemed oblivious to the energies around them. Why was I the only one who could see and sense the ghosts in the room?

The following week, I was working with one of my Reiki clients. I noticed that her brow chakra (intuitive energy center) had been closed when I had evaluated her during her last few sessions. Since I knew she meditated daily and did a lot of intuitive work, I was surprised to see this energy center closed. I told her what I was noticing and asked her what she thought about it. She explained that she was not at all surprised that her brow chakra was closed. She had been attending daily yoga classes located at a studio inside an old building, and every time she would begin to relax into the poses, ghosts would start trying to communicate with her. Eventually, she started purposely closing her brow chakra when she attended these classes so she could be free to relax without interference from spirits.

I asked her if anyone else in the class was having issues with this, and she said that yes, a few other students had commiserated with her that they had been feeling strange energy in the studio. When I asked my client if the studio owner was doing anything to clear the space, she sighed and said she had tried to talk with the owner but she just didn't get it. Eventually, my client stopped going to those classes because the energy was not beneficial for her.

I was beginning to notice a pattern. While some facilitators and location owners were doing a pristine job at setting up safe, sacred, space for their attendees, others were completely uninformed about the importance of clearing and protecting their space. This realization was brought to my attention even more with the next event I attended.

The Retreat from Hell
The event was a three-day full immersion retreat at a healing center out in the country. I had met the instructor a few times before and she seemed absolutely wonderful. In preparation for the retreat, I had been journaling and doing a lot of personal exploration into some wounds from my past. Feeling like I had already developed a level of trust in the instructor, and eager to dive into some really deep

transformation work, I allowed myself to be in an emotionally vulnerable state when I arrived for the retreat. That was a mistake on my part.

When I walked in the door, there were people busily setting up for the event, while attendees brought in their overnight bags and personal belongings. I did not know many people there, but being an independent spirit, I worked to set up my things as I anticipated the juicy transformational work we would be exploring during the weekend retreat.

To my surprise, an acquaintance I knew approached me while I was setting my suitcase on a bed. "Hi, Maya, I just want you to know that I am not okay with you being here." "Wha...?" I was puzzled. "Did I do something to offend you?" I had known Camilla to be a somewhat volatile person, but I was not aware of anything that I had done to upset her. She continued, "I arrived yesterday with the set-up crew and I just want you to know that I had to take most of that day to process my negative feelings about you with the other facilitators."

I was dumbfounded. In preparation for the retreat, I had already been doing deep emotional work that had made me emotionally tender and vulnerable. Because of my trust in the instructor, I had really let my guard down, and I had assumed it would be a safe space for me to do so. I was completely blindsided by this abrupt encounter.

Camilla turned and walked out the door and within a

split second, I was sobbing and could not stop. My head was spinning. The reality suddenly hit me. Oh my God, I have just spent half of this month's rent money on this retreat. I had made the assumption that I could let my guard down here to do some deep healing work, but I suddenly did not feel safe *at all*. I was shaking and wanted to leave. It was not just that someone had been rude. I felt like someone had just sent a hundred little daggers into my aura. I could feel that something was very wrong at this event, but I did not yet know what.

Being the open communicator that I am, I sought out the teacher whose trust had brought me to the event in the first place. I told her I was feeling emotionally unsafe, that I had concerns about the energy in this space, and I was feeling the urge to leave. I thought perhaps she could offer some insight, guidance, or even some reassurance that she would properly tend to the energy. She explained that she was not available to talk since the event was just about to start. Then, she put her hands on my shoulders, looked deeply into my eyes and asked, "Maya, do you promise to stay for the entire retreat? Do you promise not to leave?" I stammered, not feeling comfortable making such a commitment. "I promise to do what is right for me." "Okay," she said. "That is fine." She turned to attend to her work.

Soon after, the first leg of the retreat started and the students and I sat down to listen to the teacher. She went over some logistics, then explained that if we felt the urge to leave the event early, we must sit down and have a talk with her team first. We were not to leave without approval. She said, "If you leave, you will be driving home on that long highway simply bringing all your issues back home with you. You will have given up on yourself, and you will be the one responsible for that. And also, if you leave early, just know that there are no refunds, and you will have wasted your money." I sunk down in my seat. Even though things had started on a shaky foot, maybe it would get better. I tried to keep an open mind.

I listened to the class instruction, went through the group activities, and connected with some new people. When it was time for dinner, it was announced that Camilla was in charge of the kitchen and all meals throughout the weekend. "Uh-oh," I thought. I had the clear understanding that food is energy, and the nourishment I would be taking into my body all weekend would be coming directly from someone who was sending me negative energy. I tried to put it out of my mind.

The next morning, I went into Camilla's kitchen to get some breakfast. I sat down with my orange juice and tried to remain positive and courteous. Behind me, there was a conversation going on between Camilla and one of the other participants. I was shocked to hear Camilla say to the woman, "I just want you to know that I don't like you. At all. The second you walked in the door yesterday, I knew I did not like you. I'll put it plainly—I do not like other alpha-females." I saw the other woman sink down, wilting in her seat. Other people walked by to get their breakfast, and Camilla snipped at some of them, but was warm as could be to others. I sat there thinking to myself, "Oh my gosh, this is a mess!"

I didn't know why Camilla was acting this way, but in the time I had known her, I had often observed her acting rather unstable. I work to be in a place of non-judgement about people. After all, we all have things we struggle with. The problem was that the person in charge of meals for the weekend was someone who was struggling with some serious darkness. That darkness was going directly into the food, and negatively impacting the people who were eating it. As the weekend progressed, the issue seemed to get even worse. Eventually, people were complaining to the individuals in charge.

Unfortunately, the energetic chaos continued. Part of the weekend included a very intense and powerful spiritual process in which we were to release our past traumas and pain. We spent the whole day preparing for the powerful ceremony. Because of the intensity of the activity, we were split into two groups. Group A would go first, then we would take a break, then group B would go second. I was assigned to group B and was paired with a partner from group A. As the first group went through the emotional release process, the room was filled with the sounds of crying, moaning, wailing, and even screaming as group A participants released huge amounts of psychic pain. When the process was complete, we all went outside for a break before beginning the process for group B.

I knew that such powerful release work was likely to make me more vulnerable, so during the break, I slipped back inside to call in my angels and set up protection around the space where I would be sitting during the upcoming activity. When I went back outside to meet up with the group, I told the teacher that I had some concerns about the energy of our meeting space. Group A had just released huge amounts of psychic pain into the room and we would be going back into that energy. Her response was that the owners of the facility were very conservative and would absolutely not allow the burning of sage or any other herbs to clear the space. Trying to not overstep my bounds, I simply said, "Ok," and sat down. I was not in charge of the event. I did not want to be rude or bossy or attempt to take charge where it was not my place to do so, so I simply hoped for the best.

When the break was complete, I went along with the other students back to the classroom where group B proceeded to complete our powerful emotional release exercise. About halfway through, as my eyes were closed and I focused on my process, I heard Camilla, who was also in group B, let out a scream that was so loud and powerful it was more like a roar. Suddenly, I felt a huge wave of violent hatred energy surge into my aura and hit me with fierce intensity. I rolled onto my side facing away from Camilla and started sobbing. After a few more minutes, the emotional release exercise was complete.

We gathered back into our circle and proceeded with another segment of class. There was no energy clearing done on the room, nor was there any opportunity for us to clear ourselves. My head was throbbing, my body was shaking, and I was suddenly so fatigued I could barely keep my eyes open. All of my vitality had been sucked from me.

For the remaining day and a half of the event, we sat in the room that was filled with all the energy of trauma and pain we had released. Absolutely no energy clearing was done for the space or for the participants. As I tuned in with my psychic vision, I saw several hundred dark entities emerge from the shadowy woods behind the retreat center and enter into our meeting space to feed off of the residual energy of emotional anguish, and to attach energetically to the participants. Dark beings are attracted to locations where there is deep psychic pain — pain, despair, anguish, and suffering and will seek out those who are vulnerable because they are easy targets for attack, manipulation, and oppression.

At the end of the retreat, as we prepared to close out our weekend experience together, the teacher explained that it is common to feel lots of negative emotions after this retreat, including anger, depression, despair, and even violent thoughts. She said that these feelings are normal indications of the significant shifts we had initiated over the weekend. We were invited to join a private online community so we could keep in touch in the future and discuss how we were feeling.

When I got home from the retreat, I was exhausted both mentally and physically. I did some self-care and went to bed early, but I was surprised to still be utterly exhausted for the next two days. There was an extreme fatigue, brain fog, and depression that I could not shake. I knew that a lot of negative energies had attached to me during the retreat, and despite doing the standard energy clearing techniques, I just could not get back to normal.

I reached out to my own personal healing support team — three different experienced energy healers who could assist me in recovering from the after-effects of the recent retreat. All three of them corroborated what I had thought to be true — that I had not only been psychically attacked by Camilla, but that every single person at the retreat had gone home with low vibration entities attached to them.

I did not want to believe this could be true about any event for which I had had positive expectations. Not only was I certain of what I had been perceiving psychically about the event, but when three different highly experienced energy healers I truly respected could see the same thing I did, that sealed the deal. Meanwhile, I had been watching the online posts of those who had attended the group. Many were reporting exactly what the teacher had predicted — anger, depression, rage, and more — and the teacher was responding to each of them, telling them it was all a normal part of the process. And yet, when my team and I tuned into what was happening to the members, we could see that they were each being oppressed and attacked by the dark entities that had come home with them. It was alarming to witness, and even more alarming to see that the instructor was oblivious to what was really going on.

Shortly after, I wrote a short and respectfully worded letter stating that as part of my self-care I was choosing to remove myself from the online group. I did not explain why, but simply stated it was something I needed to do at this time to take good care of myself. I sent this to both the instructor and the group with my well-meaning positive wishes for the group.

The instructor did follow up with me and asked if I would give some specific feedback. Honestly, I was so shocked and mortified by the chaos of the event that I did not feel comfortable telling her the actual specifics of why I had removed myself. Instead, my response was more general. I told her that I did not feel that adequate care had been taken to clear and protect the space and the participants. I told her that I feel it is of the utmost importance that the instructor be the one to set the precedent of the energy climate of their class. I felt she had not done this, and that in fact, someone else's energy (Camilla's) had been running the show, causing a great deal of unnecessary energetic chaos throughout the event. After removing myself completely from the group, it took about two weeks to clear all of the negative energetic after-effects.

I took some vital lessons away from that retreat which became clearer to me over the next few weeks. First, I had been entirely too *nice*. (I'm sure you were already thinking that several pages ago!) I realized that throughout my childhood, as well as within my current spiritual community, I had consistently been taught to give my power away to whomever was in charge and to refrain from speaking up if it might make waves. I realized that I had been abdicating my power to anyone in authority, assuming they were going to take good care of me and my surroundings, to ensure the safety of me and those around me. The truth is that those in authority — facilitators, studio owners, spiritual leaders, and teachers — will sometimes fall short. Blindly trusting anyone is a huge mistake. No matter how popular the authority figure is, how many books they have written, how spiritual they may seem, or how many students or followers they have, you absolutely cannot assume they are doing what is necessary to protect your energy. Your protection is up to you.

One of the most important lessons I learned was that it is important to *speak up* when something is not right. It does not matter if anyone thinks I am being rude or bossy for doing so, or if they think I am crazy, or overreacting, or off my rocker. The truth is, I can see things many others cannot, and if I do not speak up, the problem will persist. Not only will it negatively impact me, but also those around me if I do not speak up!

Another important realization was that if something does not feel good to me, I have every right to remove myself from that space. It does not matter one bit if people think I am being rude or over-reactive or if they do not understand why I am leaving. And it also does not matter if I will have to forfeit what I paid for the event. Not only that, I do not need the facilitator's approval to leave.

I'll note here that one of the reasons I stayed for the entire retreat was because I had made a commitment, not only to the facilitator, but to myself. I had made a personal commitment to go through the process of that retreat. If I left early, I would be breaking a commitment to myself and others. And then who would I be? Undependable and a quitter? Well, in the aftermath of that retreat, I realized that I indeed *do* have the right to revoke any and all commitments, agreements, and promises if at any time I realize that I am unsafe physically or energetically. In the future, I will sure as heck either speak up or leave if I am in any way feeling unsafe.

In fact, a year after learning this lesson, I put it into action. I was signed up to attend an overnight healing dance ritual with a local spiritual teacher. As someone who loves healing dance, I was really excited for this event, but as the date drew near I became increasing more anxious. Something felt wrong to me about the event and I felt that I would be vulnerable to some negative energies especially while I would be sleeping outside out on the land. Each day, my feelings grew stronger and my anxiety grew. I recognized that I was receiving important information from my 'inner guidance system' to keep me safe, so I decided to heed the warning. Three days before the event I contacted the teacher and told her that I would not be attending due to some private reasons. This meant that I would be forfeiting my class fee, and I told her I was okay with that. My safety was more important than the money. And so, I skipped the event and felt very good about my decision to do so.

Seeking Answers

By this time, I was certainly noticing the growing number of troubling instances that were showing up in my world. I was still filled with a lot of self-doubt and did not understand why I was having these experiences while everyone else seemed just fine. Seeking some guidance, I decided to attend a local psychic fair occurring that weekend. Michelle, an acquaintance I had met a couple of years prior, was going to be there doing readings. She had been a beam of love and light at a time when I had really been struggling. We had connected as colleagues and had maintained a minor connection via social media. I remembered her as being a positive and spirit-led woman, and so I hoped she would have some positive insights and perspective about my recent experiences.

When I arrived at the fair, I walked straight to her booth. I was a woman on a mission. We gave each other a big hug and engaged in some friendly chitchat. She said that she was hoping that the fair would be slow because she was really tired and not quite in the mood for a full day of doing psychic readings. Her energy looked different than I had remembered it. It looked like she had a dark cloud hovering over her head and back. I brushed it off, assuming that maybe she was just tired, and told her I was interested in a psychic reading. We sat down and I proceeded to tell her about some of the experiences I had been having lately, about how shocked I was about the negative energies I was seeing and how most people could not see what I could see. By that time, I was desperate to find someone who would tell me what was going on and give me some comfort.

I got quite the opposite. After Michelle listened to my stories, she took a deep breath and looked right at me. "Maya, you are drawing these experiences to you because of some negativity deep within you. Because of your negative thinking, you are manifesting these things in your world." "Hmm," I said. "Go on." "Well, Maya, I've got to say that you're pretty paranoid." She shifted in her seat, looking a little self-conscious. "I've only had one other client as paranoid as you and she was paranoid to the extreme."

We finished up the intuitive reading, and I thanked her as I thought about what she had said. As soon as I stood up and walked away, I suddenly realized, "Oh my gosh! I feel even *more* confused than before, and even worse! Ugh!" I walked to the bathroom to freshen up and clear my head. I went to the sink and turned the water on. As soon as I put my hands under the running water, I suddenly felt my spirit guide, Isabel, by my side and she gave me an instantaneous message that was crystal clear.

"Maya! You keep looking for answers outside of yourself rather than looking within. We have purposely sent people into your world who would give you false and confusing information so that you would finally understand this message. Please stop looking to others who do *not* have the answers for you. You already have the truth within you. You must begin to finally trust yourself."

As I strolled back into the fair, I realized I had ignored overt signs that Michelle was not receiving clear messages. She had outright told me she was exhausted and not in the mood to do readings that day, not to mention the dark cloud of energy that had been surrounding her and impeding her ability to see clearly. I didn't fault her for this, because we all have days when we are tired and our energy is not so great.

I thought about my spirit guide, Isabel, and the importance of her message. I took a deep breath. It was time for me to start trusting myself. For my entire life, I had been placing my faith in others more than I had been trusting myself, and it was time to shift that old deeply ingrained habit. I knew that the things I was seeing and experiencing were very real, and I vowed that from now on I would trust myself implicitly.

A few weeks later I scheduled myself to receive a long-distance energy healing session with Karie, who had been doing sessions for me for over ten years. She had helped me through many of my life transitions and spiritual growth spurts. During the session, she did some deep clearing and healing and shared some messages she was receiving for me. I told her about all of the shocking experiences I had been having lately. With the utmost compassion, she explained that I was spiritually evolving from third dimensional consciousness up to fourth dimensional consciousness and it would take a little getting used to. Essentially, my vibration was raising more and more, which was further opening my intuition and abilities. She said that this transition can be difficult for some. All of that made sense to me.

I asked her if there is anything I should do about the situations I had been witnessing. Should I get involved? Karie explained that I was correct in my perceptions. I was not, in fact, paranoid, or causing these negative events, as Michelle had previously hypothesized. Rather, these situations were being placed in front of me because I was supposed to assist in shifting the energy. She said that because I can see things others cannot, I am responsible for stepping in to assist those who are vulnerable when it is called for. Karie explained that in the future, when I am in a situation where I become aware of negative energies, I need to take a moment to tap into Divine guidance. As I tune into spirit, it will become clear to me if I am supposed to either speak directly to whomever is in charge, assist by working quietly to shift the energies, or do nothing. Once I receive my answer, I am to proceed accordingly. Her advice helped me tremendously. In the past when I would observe negative energies, I had been caught between shock and inaction because I was so careful of not overstepping my bounds or stepping on any toes at other people's events. I finally understood that it is my responsibility to speak up and help in certain situations, and I have applied that principle ever since.

LESSON 2 – TRUST YOUR INTUITION & THE FIVE "CLAIRS"

Many people I meet tell me they believe they are not psychic, and that only a few select people are born with this gift. That is simply not true. All people are born with a natural intuitive ability. While some are born with a stronger ability than others, the truth is that every single person can learn to develop and strengthen their psychic skills.

Strong intuition is a vital part of healthy psychic self-defense. If you can sense the energies around you, you can judge which energies are beneficial for you and which are not. And then, with the information in later chapters, you will also learn techniques for clearing and protecting yourself. With a stronger intuition, you will be able to tell if a person, situation, or location is a good fit for you, and you will be able to protect yourself from the things that are not healthy for you.

Overall, the very best way to enhance your intuition is to develop a clear and quiet mind that is free of chatter, stress, and worry. Easier said than done, I know, but developing a peaceful mind will also help to reduce your stress, improve your well-being, and enhance your happiness. The best way to quiet your mind is to set aside at least ten minutes each day to sit in meditation, prayer, contemplation, or gratitude. If your life is so busy that you do not feel you have time to do this, then you need it even more! You will feel so much better and clearer, and your mental focus and productivity will go up, making that ten minutes each day worth your while.

In addition to a daily meditation, you can practice being more aware of your thoughts, emotions, and other sensations throughout the day. Most people receive psychic information all day long, but they are too busy, they are not paying attention, and their mind is too full of chatter to even notice the information trying to come through. So, remember this: You are already psychic. You just have to start paying better attention so you can receive the messages. Take a moment to check in with yourself several times a day. How are you feeling? What are you thinking? Are you getting any 'nudges' about anything? Are you getting a good feeling or bad feeling about a person or situation? Those are all aspects of your intuition, so do not discount any of it. Keep an open mind. You can even jot down the information you receive so you do not forget.

As you develop your psychic skill set, you will also learn to trust yourself more. For your own psychic protection, it is crucial that you learn to trust yourself implicitly so that you never give your power away to any person or entity that does not have your best interest at heart. In the following section, I will go through each type of intuitive sense, along with suggestions on how to develop each one. Just like any new skill, it takes time and ongoing practice to develop and strengthen your abilities. Be patient, have an open mind, and stay committed to practicing and exploring these aptitudes on an ongoing basis.

TYPES OF INTUITION

The first five types of intuition correspond with your five physical senses: sight, hearing, touch, taste, and smell, and the sixth type of intuition relates to your inner knowing. Each type of intuition can be experienced either internally or externally, as I will explain below. After each description, I have included a few suggestions to strengthen the detailed psychic ability. Advanced psychic development is beyond the scope of this book; however, the exercises below will help you to develop a solid foundation.

Most people are strongest in one psychic modality, so do not be concerned if you do not have strong abilities in all of them. As you read through the list, you might be able to identify which ones are your primary and secondary strengths. A rare number of people are adept at all of these senses. This type of person is called a 'bridge.'

Note: If you have any history of mental health issues, please consult your medical provider before proceeding with any intuitive development exercises.

1. Clairvoyance (psychic sight)

Clairvoyance, also known as 'clear sight,' is the ability to receive psychic information through your sense of vision. As an internal ability, the information is seen in the mind's eye. As an external ability, the information is seen outside of oneself, as in the case of seeing a ghost in your room. Examples of clairvoyance would include being able to see energy, aura colors, spirits, angels, or any other information through the sense of vision. Those strong in clairvoyance will have these experiences either internally, externally, or as a combination of both. You may also see flashes of past, present, or future either in your mind's eye or as a movie playing out before your eyes.

Psychic development exercises:
The best way to develop your inner clairvoyance is to practice your visualization skills. Close your eyes and begin by visualizing different colors one at a time. I recommend using the card deck, "The Secret Language of Color Cards" by Inna Segal. With the deck, you can gaze at each color with your eyes open, then close your eyes to visualize the color in your mind's eye. Practice this with as many colors as you wish. If you do not have the card deck, you can also do it by looking at different colors in your environment or even doing an online Google search for various colors to gaze at.

Once you have practiced visualizing colors, you can then practice visualizing simple objects, like an apple, chair, plant, flower, or glass of water, then move to more complex things like visualizing a person, a mountain, a house, an animal, an ornate object, etc. From there, you can even take yourself on a guided visualization where you imagine walking or traveling on a journey and observing everything you see along the way.

You can also do exercises to improve your external clairvoyance. Remember, external clairvoyance is when you see things in front of you with your eyes open. As such, you will also practice this skill with your eyes open. Unless you have a natural tendency for it, external clairvoyance can be a bit more difficult to develop compared to internal clairvoyance, but with practice you will gradually be able to develop these skills. The key to external clairvoyance is to allow your gaze to soften because you will not be focusing in the way you normally do to read a book or look at objects in your world.

Instead, allow your eyes to go out of focus by relaxing your gaze. (If you wear glasses, take them off.) Your vision may become fuzzy or blurry, and that is what you want. Allow yourself to blink naturally whenever you need to as you continue to hold this soft gaze. Try this relaxed gaze technique while staring at a house plant, tree, or flower. Optimal conditions would include soft lighting with no harsh shadows. Over time, you may be able to see the aura (energy field) of the plant or even energy pouring out of it. For most people, the aura may look like a shadow or soft light surrounding the object, while those gifted in this area will be able to see specific colors.

To see your own aura, set your hand, palm down, in front of you with the fingers spread open against a plain white surface. Gently gaze at the space between your fingers until your eyes go out of focus. To see another person's aura, have them sit in front of a white wall or curtain. Gaze at their third eye (the space between their brows on their forehead) and as your eyes gently go out of focus, allow your peripheral vision to notice any shadow or light surrounding the person's head. As you practice working with your own aura or that of another person, you will eventually be able to see a layer of shadow or white light surrounding the edges of the physical body, and in some cases, you will be able to see color.

2. Clairaudience (psychic hearing)

Clairaudience, also known as "clear hearing" is the ability to receive psychic information through your sense of hearing. As an internal ability, you may hear a voice in your own mind, and it may either sound like your own voice or like someone else's voice. Many people invalidate information that is heard in their own voice because they figure it is just their own mind making things up. Do not discount information received in your own voice because, more times than not, it is completely valid intuitive information you are receiving. As an external ability, the information is heard in a similar way to hearing someone in the same room speaking into your ear. Externally, you may hear a voice saying your name or sharing a word or message. You may hear whispers, animal noises, bumps or knocks, or any number of sounds, so this ability is not just limited to human speech. Hearing high or low pitch frequencies can also be a sign of entity activity, where the lower pitch can be a sign of low vibration (evil) beings, and higher pitch can be a sign of either genuine high vibration beings like angels or it can indicate that false light entities are present.

Psychic Development Exercises:
Developing your internal clairaudience is pretty straightforward. You will want to start with simple, short auditory messages to get your mind used to receiving messages in this way. Think of saying the word "yes" in your mind. You are not saying the word aloud, but strongly and clearly in your mind. Try this a few times. Now try it with the word "no." Repeat a few times in your mind with conviction. Now try it with the word "maybe." The goal here is to program your mind to receive auditory messages in your own voice. Now try some other words or phrases, like "opportunity," "not now," "be careful," "now is the time," etc. I recommend using the card deck, Angel Answers Oracle Cards, by Radleigh Valentine. Each card has a different short message, like the examples above, to give you many different auditory messages to practice.

To develop your external clairaudience, it is imperative that you become accustomed to being in a quiet environment for at least part of your day. If you are someone who always has to have your radio or television playing in the background and your auditory senses are always receiving stimuli, it will be much more difficult for the channels to be open to receive auditory messages. Try sitting in silence for at least ten minutes a day, or completing your daily tasks like washing the dishes, folding laundry, cooking, exercising, etc. in total silence or with soft, unobtrusive instrumental music. The quieter your environment, the easier it will be to hear intuitive messages when they try to come through.

3. Clairsentience (psychic feeling)

Clairsentience, also known as 'clear feeling' is the ability to receive psychic information through the sense of touch. Internal clairsentience occurs when you feel a sensation within your body which is giving you some sort of signal or message. For example, you may feel light-headed, dizzy, or shaky, or you may notice a headache, pain or tension in your body, a tightening or knot in your stomach, or any other sensations to give you the signal that something in your environment is not right. Similarly, your body may feel relaxed, your mind clear, and your heart open when you are in a situation that is safe and right for you. Internal clairsentience is also commonly related to psychic empathy, the ability to feel other people's physical symptoms and/or emotions in your own body. Some empaths can also pick up on the feelings and sensations of animals, plant life, natural disasters or human-made disasters on the planet, and even feelings of whole groups of people, like a city, country, or particular population experiencing discord or suffering.

External clairsentience involves the ability to psychically receive information via your sense of touch on your skin. These sensations may include goosebumps, the hair standing up on the back of your neck, cold shivers, temperature fluctuations, pressure on a part of your body, or any number of physical sensations which may be signaling to you about the energies in your environment. Many people report one or more of the above physical sensations when they are visited by a spiritual being such as a benign ghost or even a low vibration being such as a malicious ghost or demon.

External clairsentience also includes the ability to sense energy with your hands. Many Reiki practitioners and other types of spiritual healers have the ability to use their hands to sense any imbalances, blockages, pain, and more in a person's aura, chakras, and physical body. The practitioner may feel sensations of hot, cold, tingling, pulsating, pressure, pain, and more in their hands.

Another aspect of external clairsentience involves the ability called psychometry. Psychometry is the ability to hold an object, and through the sense of touch, be able to intuitively pick up information about that object. Metal tends to hold onto its prior vibrations and history, which is why many psychics who are reading a person will ask to hold a piece of jewelry that the person often wore. Of course, any object can be intuitively read through psychometry, but metal objects will tend to provide the strongest information.

Psychic Development Exercises:
To get in touch with your internal clairsentience, you will want to practice becoming more aware of the sensations in your body. Many people nowadays are quite disconnected from their physical body and are living almost entirely inside their head. To connect with your inner psychic feeling, you must reconnect with your body. Each day take a few moments to close your eyes, breathe gently, and bring your awareness to different areas of your body, first your head, then

shoulders, arms, hands, chest and upper back, abdomen and mid-back, pelvis and low back, hips, thighs, knees, lower legs, then feet. Take as much time as you need to tune into any physical or emotional sensations in each area. Does that area feel relaxed, tense, open, closed, painful, comfortable, warm, cool, etc.? When you tune into this part of your body, do you feel stressed, calm, sad, happy, nervous, confident, etc.?

When you get used to tuning into the signals within your own body, you will also develop the ability to identify when the physical sensations you are feeling are not your own. There is a simple question you can ask yourself. "Is this feeling mine?" Then, feel into your body and recognize if that sensation had been there previously or if it came on suddenly out of the blue. If it came on suddenly without any prior history of this issue, that is a sign that you are receiving clairsentient information from your environment. With practice, you will be able to ascertain if the physical sensation is actually yours, or if it is being caused by receiving psychic information about someone or something in the environment around you.

Once you determine that the feeling is not yours, you can take a breath and notice the environment around you. Consider where the feeling might be coming from and what this sensation might be telling you. For example, you are in a meeting and you suddenly notice your head begins to throb with pain. True, you could actually have a normal everyday headache. On the other hand, you might be picking up on someone else's headache, or you may be receiving information that something about this situation is not good for you. With practice, you will be able to interpret these signals more and more clearly. If at any time you are receiving sensations that are making you feel ill or do not feel good to you, you can quickly and easily release any physical sensations that do not belong to you. With conviction, simply say this statement, "I release all energies that do not belong to me." Take a deep breath, blow it out, and know that you are the master of your own energy.

Developing your external clairsentience is quite fun. To strengthen this sense, practice touching a variety of different objects around your home. Touch each object and notice the temperature, texture, and feel. You can even pet your cat or dog. In this practice you are getting used to tuning in to the sensations received through the palms of your hands. To tune in even more to your sense of touch, practice touching objects with your eyes closed.

Now, practice sensing energy with your hands. Vigorously rub the palms of your hands together to generate some heat. Pull your hands apart, then face your palms toward one another and carefully tune into any sensations you feel in each hand. Try holding your hands about twelve inches apart and notice how your hands feel. Do you feel heat, pressure, coolness, tingling, or pushing away or pulling together of the hands? Now move your hands about six inches apart and notice how your hands feel. Now try pushing your hands even closer.

You can also practice this same exercise with a friend. Rub your own hands together, then stand apart from each other about twelve inches, palms facing the other person, and notice how the energy feels coming from the other person's hands. Be sure to share what you are sensing. Then, move closer and practice some more.

You can also take this exercise a step further by holding your palms between one to twelve inches away from a person, pet, or plant, and notice any sensations you feel in your hands. If you are practicing with a person, have them relax in a chair or on a couch, bed, or massage table while you gently move your hands through their energy field to feel their energy. If you are working with a pet, be sure to honor the pet's space, as some animals love this practice, while others do not. As you practice, the sensations in your hands may be subtle, so pay close attention.

4. Clairolfaction (psychic smell)
Clairolfaction is the ability to receive psychic information through the sense of smell. Internal clairolfaction occurs when you get the sense of a smell within your mind, while external clairolfaction gives the sensation of smelling something in the surrounding environment. With internal psychic smell, you might suddenly be filled with the memory of an ex-lover's cologne, and with external psychic smell, you will actually smell the scent even though no one in the room is actually wearing that fragrance.

On one occasion, I suddenly picked up on the strong fragrance of roses, even though there were no roses anywhere to be seen. It definitely did not smell like perfume or essential oil, but rather, as though someone was literally holding a bouquet of roses right under my nose. The scent of roses has a specific spiritual meaning for me, so I immediately recognized I was receiving a message via external clairolfaction.

Psychic smell (internal or external) can occur when spiritual beings are nearby. Some ascended masters (very holy beings) can make their presence known through the scent of roses or other floral scents. A loved one in spirit form can make their presence known by sending a scent associated with them, like their perfume or cologne, or even the cookies they used to bake for you. Negative entities can make their presence known through foul smells that have no other physical origin.

Psychic Development Exercises:
The key to developing your clairolfaction is to tune into your sense of physical smell. Have fun sniffing different things that have strong, distinct fragrances, for example, oranges, chocolate, different types of flowers, spices, and essential oils. Between smelling each thing, you can sniff a small jar of coffee beans to reset your olfactory senses, and then go on to smelling the next thing. Note that your sense of physical smell will be inhibited if you have a cold, allergies, or any type of sinus issue, though this will not in any way inhibit your ability to psychically smell. Remember that the very best way to tap into any of your psychic senses is to practice paying attention. A prime example of clairolfaction is when a fragrance suddenly pops into

your mind for no identifiable reason and it makes you think of a person or situation. The person may be thinking of you, they may be going through an important life transition, or they may be in need of assistance. Whatever the reason, be sure to pay attention and receive it as important psychic information.

5. Clairgustance (psychic taste)
Clairgustance, or psychic taste, is the least common of the psychic senses, but it is still important to acknowledge. Internal clairgustance occurs when you get a sense of a particular taste within your mind, and external clairgustance occurs when you experience an actual taste within your mouth. Examples might include experiencing the memory of the flavors of a special dish a deceased loved one used to prepare, or feeling an unpleasant taste in your mouth when you encounter negative energies.

Psychic Development Exercises:
The simple way to enhance your external clairgustance is to tune into your physical sense of taste. Experiment with tasting different flavors on your tongue, including sweet, salty, sour, bitter, and savory. Take note of how each food may include hints of one or more of the above flavors, and notice how each food and corresponding flavor makes you feel. To practice your internal clairgustance, you can use your imagination to invoke each flavor. In this instance, without actually eating anything, you are going to imagine eating each food one at a time, focusing on the flavors and textures in your mouth. In this way, you will be tapping into

this sense in a new way, which will allow you to better recognize when information comes through your psychic channels via the sense of taste.

6. Claircognizance (psychic knowing)

Claircognizance, or 'psychic knowing,' is the ability to know things due to receiving information through your intuition. There's no practical reason why you know the information; *You just know*. With claircognizance, you don't see a vision, hear a message, feel information in your body, or smell or taste the information. With psychic knowing, you simply *know* the information. When you meet someone, you instantly know whether they can or cannot be trusted. When embarking on a new project, you simply know whether it will or will not work out. When you meet the love of your life, you instantly know that he or she is the one. When driving, you simply know that you are supposed to take a different route (and later find out there was an accident on your usual route).

When you immediately know whether someone is lying or telling you the truth, or simply know information about a person or situation without any other discernable reason for knowing it (and it is not coming through one of your other psychic senses), you are experiencing claircognizance.

Psychic Development Exercises:
To enhance your claircognizant abilities, pay attention to your thoughts and feelings. When you have the thought, "That is/isn't going to work out," or "They can/cannot be trusted," or "This situation isn't safe,"

etc., be sure to pay attention to those psychic knowings. Many people experience claircognizance every day, but they write it off, assuming it is just their overactive imagination or a paranoid mind. Yet others do acknowledge and heed the information they are receiving, but they take it for granted, not giving themselves credit for the psychic abilities that are coming through loud and clear, continuing to tell themselves that they are not actually psychic. In short, be sure to pay attention to your inner voice and feelings, and acknowledge the claircognizance you are already experiencing.

OTHER METHODS OF INTUITION

The six intuitive senses described above are the primary ways that psychic information can be obtained through your senses. These senses can be experienced one at a time or in a variety of combinations. Consider dreams, for an example. While in a sleeping state, your dreams may include visions, auditory messages, physical sensations, and more, providing you with psychic information about a situation, or even a premonition of future events. Another example would be channeling, in which a person opens themselves up to receive messages from a spirit guide or ascended master. These messages can be received through images, auditory messages, receiving an 'instant download' of the message (clear knowing), and more.

A third example is the use of oracle cards. Oracle cards are quite popular these days and can include tarot cards, angel cards, fairy cards, and many other themes. The inquirer can shuffle the cards face down and use their intuition to pick one or more to flip over and interpret. I have a friend who says she feels a tickle in the palm of her hand when she moves her hand over the card she is supposed to pick. On the contrary, when I use oracle cards, I depend on my sense of psychic knowing to tell me which cards to pick. Each card has an image and/or message, and the person reading the cards may use their intuitive skills to fill more detail into the meaning and message of each card. Some who use oracle cards simply read the corresponding message with each card; however, the optimal way to use oracle cards is to also allow your various intuitive senses to fill in the message for you.

There are numerous methods in which your intuitive skills can be applied. Going into a comprehensive explanation of them would be beyond the scope of this book but referring to the above examples should help to get you started.

TRUST YOURSELF

Now that you have learned about each intuitive sense — clairvoyance, clairaudience, clairsentience, clairolfaction, clairgustance, and claircognizance, it is time to go through the psychic development exercises above to work on developing your skills. Simply reading these pages will not develop your intuition.

You must practice. The more you practice, the stronger and clearer your psychic abilities will become, and the better you will be able to identify and follow intuitive information when you receive it. As you develop your abilities, you will also gain trust in yourself and the information you are receiving. With self-trust comes the ability to discern the energies around you in order to keep yourself and your loved ones safe.

CHAPTER 3 – THE BEGINNING OF IT ALL

It is now time to delve into the chain of events that led to the extreme psychic attack I experienced in the spring of 2016. The attack itself was multi-layered and involved different storylines interwoven together, with spiritual assault coming from more than one source. The story is fascinating, complex, and intriguing, and as the details unfold, a great deal of useful information about psychic protection is revealed. This part of my story begins with an exploration of how sexual predators (and energy predators in general) are able to manipulate the energy of their victims. We will explore a multitude of other types of psychic attack as my story unfolds in the chapters that follow.

The Women's Healing Circle

It was late April when I received a mysterious message from my colleague, Elizabeth. Her vague message only said that I was invited to participate in a private meeting regarding an important community matter. When I saw the message, my stomach turned. My gut was telling me that the mysterious meeting was probably going to be related to the issue of sexual predators working within our spiritual healing community.

Elizabeth and I had worked with this issue several years prior, along with the assistance of other very concerned, heart-centered women and men. At that time, Elizabeth and I, in addition to others in the community, had helped to form a healing circle for women who had been harmed by male healers. These individuals had used their positions of power to manipulate their clients into sexual relationships.

To clarify, I believe that there has been a long history in our world of both female and male healing practitioners and spiritual teachers misusing their power and manipulating clients for their own self-interest. In fact, I have personally witnessed spiritual teachers of all genders and orientations who used energetic and magickal practices to keep their students small and disempowered. Based on the teacher's insecurities and need to feed their ego, they create a scenario where the student remains dependent upon them, and the teacher attempts to keep the student from ever meeting their highest potential. In doing so, the spiritual teacher can always remain the big kahuna with many needy, devoted followers falling all over them in admiration. Behind this scenario is energetic manipulation in which the person in leadership manipulates their followers and sources energy from them, too.

The manipulator and perpetrator scenario has never been purely a male issue. It is a temptation for all human beings in leadership roles. There are many amazing healers and spiritual teachers in this world. And unfortunately, there are also human beings who choose to use their gifts to harm rather than heal. In regards to abuse of a sexual nature, since I was working primarily with women in my healing practice at the time, most of my experience was focused on helping women heal from abuse by men. I also recognize and believe that in the right context, sexual energy can be used for beneficial healing; however, if it is not approached with the utmost integrity in the appropriate circumstances, it can cause great harm.

It became quite evident that the issue of practitioner abuse in my healing community needed serious attention. The women's healing circle that was formed allowed each woman to share her story within the safe and loving environment we had created. Each woman in the circle had expressed her own unique experience of manipulation at the hands of her so-called healer. Some of the women were too afraid to share the name of their abuser, expressing trepidation that there would be backlash from the perpetrator, while others spoke openly and shared names, knowing they were in a safe space to do so. Within the private circle, eight different male perpetrators were identified, some of them local and some of them in other cities, making it abundantly clear that this issue is most certainly widespread in many communities.

It was heartbreaking to hear each woman weep as she shared her own personal, private story. Some of the women expressed a certain level of confusion and self-blame (as do many victims), believing they were somehow at fault for causing or allowing the abuse. One of the women in attendance had a developmental disability. She was quite young and was still a virgin when her spiritual teacher convinced her to begin a sexual relationship with him. She was one of over twenty-five women who had been manipulated in such a way by this particular teacher who had the practice of surrounding himself with very young women that he would 'mentor.'

In all of the cases, it was clear how each perpetrator had spent time 'grooming' his victims, taking whatever time was needed to establish the victim's trust through manipulative means. For one of our meetings, we had an absolutely wonderful, compassionate, caring guest presenter who was a therapist with experience and expertise in helping clients who had been abused by their healing practitioner. One of the most important things that she helped the women to understand is that what happened to them was not their fault. She explained that the person in the helping role, whether it is a massage therapist, energy healer, spiritual teacher, church clergy, therapist, doctor, legal counsel, or etc., by default are in a position of power over their client. It is up to the 'helping professional' to maintain professional ethics at all times and to never use their position of power to manipulate their client for their own personal gain, be it sexual, financial, or otherwise.

The intent of the group was to allow the women a space to feel heard, understood, and supported without judgement, to create a space where healing could begin to occur for them, and to help to educate the community about the issue. Overall, the group was a success in that it allowed a safe container for those who needed it. However, despite the positive and loving intent of all involved in the group, there was serious negative backlash from our local spiritual community.

Both the female victims and the women assisting them were demonized and shamed. Many in the community were shockingly unsupportive of the victims. In fact, several community members even stood up to support the perpetrators, stating that all the women were lying and were on some kind of hateful "witch hunt" against all men. It was so appalling to witness the women who had already been victimized, being victimized once again through the outright lack of support from their community. Many of the women felt betrayed and some expressed that they would never publicly report what had happened to them for fear of further backlash from the community. The situation itself certainly mirrored the 'rape culture' in our society, in which victims are blamed and perpetrators are praised and supported.

I was so exceedingly disappointed in my own spiritual community when all of this happened. My eyes were truly opened to the level of 'spiritual dysfunction' taking place, the outright act of using spiritual teachings as a means to avoid and deflect dealing with serious issues and real emotions. Each time we reached out to our community for help, we received comments like this:

"We can't help with this issue because that's THEIR negative karma, and if we get involved, we'll be taking on that negative karma as well."

"These women are not my own students/clients, so it is none of my business. I don't want to get involved."

"Those women had a soul contract to be a victim in this lifetime and therefore we cannot interfere."

"These women need to just let it go. Forgive and forget. Stop fixating on this so much. Embrace unconditional love. The men need our unconditional love, support, and forgiveness."

"You women are leading a witch hunt against these men. You're on an angry vendetta and we won't support that."

One spiritual leader in our community even said to me, *"Maya, this issue is about you, so the solution is to look within and simply focus on your own healing, rather than working directly with the community issue. Work on your own issues regarding men, and that will heal this community issue."*

I should note that our group was not in any way about anger and revenge, but rather, about creating a safe, nurturing, loving space where the women could share their story and feel heard, acknowledged, and understood. Our other goal was to help raise awareness in our community so we could encourage healing for all parties. Unfortunately, many people in our community were engaging in forms of 'spiritual dysfunction' techniques so they could stay within their safe spiritual bubble and avoid dealing with an uncomfortable and difficult issue.

Somehow our positive, healing intent was not seen or understood by many in our community. The needs of the victims were ignored, and the women were told they were wrong and unloving for seeking healing and support. Meanwhile, some of the male perpetrators chose to spread false rumors about the group. Rather than stepping forward, acknowledging the truth of what they had done, apologizing, and taking honest steps to heal themselves and the situation, they instead created a smokescreen. One of the patterns I came to observe over the years was that when any type of perpetrator is trying to cover their tracks, they will often utilize the tactic of gaslighting. Essentially, they create a smokescreen story that says that *they* are the victim in this, that people are making things up about them and they don't know why. The perpetrators are so convincing in their manipulative storytelling that they end up convincing people to staunchly defend the perpetrator and speak out against the victims. At first, I was confused and hurt when the perpetrators began spreading horrible rumors. Over time, though, I saw this tactic used again and again by those exhibiting sociopathic behavior, and I came to understand that it is the technique they use to deflect people from the truth. Unfortunately, this tactic works all too well.

The situation was traumatic for the female victims, not only because of what they had experienced with a healing practitioner they had trusted, but also because their own community had let them down. It was really heartbreaking to observe all of it. At the same time, I went through my own personal trauma. I was the main target for most of the backlash from the community. The perpetrators were focusing most of their gas-lighting tactics towards *me*. I'm not sure why I was targeted so vehemently or why the other circle facilitators were left alone for the most part. Perhaps it was because I was already a more well-known figure in the community, so maybe I was the easiest, most visible target. At any rate, it was very stressful, scary, and upsetting to witness people spreading horrible, untrue rumors about me and harming my reputation. My business and my livelihood were still recovering after the 2009 economic crash and I was afraid this situation would end up causing me irreparable harm. I had already lost nearly everything in 2009 and I was still in quite a vulnerable position. I did not need to go through that kind of loss again, especially when there were several highly qualified people in our community who could assist with this issue. Shortly thereafter, I made the difficult decision to resign my position as one of the co-facilitators. The woman I suggested to take my place did a wonderful job. With her contributions, as well as the contributions of others, the group was able to meet several more times for some powerful, profound healing.

Getting More Information

With all of that in my past experience, when I got the vague message from Elizabeth about an important "community issue," it naturally brought up some trepidation about getting involved. I thought, "Oh God, not this. I don't think I can deal with it again." I replied to the group message, telling them that I was not sure I wanted to attend, that I needed more information and I needed to check in with my inner guidance. I had a feeling the issue involved someone I knew and had history with. When I tuned into the situation, I could sense a complicated drama web with the people involved and the people wanting to discuss the issue.

My intent was to stay out of any unnecessary drama, so I was pretty certain I was going to stay uninvolved with the issue this time around.

Yet, being the open communicator that I am, I figured that a one-on-one phone call with Elizabeth would help give me more information so I could make an informed decision about the level of involvement I would choose. Elizabeth was not available for a phone call until later in the week but Anne was available that night. Anne was one of the people who had been included in the message, and she apparently was privy to whatever was going on. I had known Anne for a few months. She had come to a couple of my energy healing certification classes and she was planning to apply those new credentials to opening a healing center of her own. I had also recently attended the planning meeting for her new healing arts center, located not far from where I was living at the time, and where several energy healers were in attendance sharing their services.

Anne and I exchanged a couple of messages and made arrangements for a phone call. During the call, she explained to me that there were some concerns about one of the healers who had attended her recent planning meeting at her center. Anne explained that during the event, a healing practitioner named Jeffrey had been sharing energy balancing sessions with some of the attendees. (I remembered this, because I had politely declined a session with him.) Jennifer, one of the guests, reported that partway through receiving her healing session, she had opened her eyes to see a demon's face with glowing red eyes superimposed over Jeffrey's face. Jennifer is an adept clairvoyant and healer, and she was quite convinced that Jeffrey had a demon working with him. Anne wanted to know what I thought about this, if I agreed with Jennifer's assessment, and whether she should ask Jeffrey to no longer do sessions at her healing center.

"Oh, jeez," I thought, sighing loudly. I had already suspected the current "important community issue" was about Jeffrey. I had had my own unsavory experiences with him a few years prior, although different in nature compared to Jennifer's experience. In addition to my own personal experiences, I had also observed some disturbing things about how Jeffrey was manipulating energy with his clients.

I replied to Anne, "Let me think for just a moment how I want to respond to this."

Holding my phone in one hand, I shook my head, thinking silently, "Please, God, leave me out of this. I don't want to get involved, especially when it's related to this particular person!"

The Cords That Bind Us

My mind flashed back to meeting Jeffrey at a local spiritual event and how we had developed a close friendship over the course of three years. During that time, our friendship had been completely platonic, and I had zero romantic interest in him whatsoever. We were simply buddies.

With no warning, three years into our friendship things suddenly changed. We had exchanged energy healing sessions with one another at my home. During my years as an energy healer, I had exchanged services with personal friends on many occasions; however, this was the first time Jeffrey and I had done so. Within the next twenty-four hours after our shared sessions, I began having obsessive sexual thoughts about him. I was surprised by this because, first of all, it was unusual for me to have such intense impulses about anything, and second, I had never thought of Jeffrey in that way. I had been single for a couple of years, and he had recently gone through a divorce. I was not certain where these feelings were coming from, but I began to wonder if maybe it was time for me to consider him for a possible romantic relationship.

The next time he came to my house for a visit, he started flirting with me right off the bat. I am a very intentional person about everything in my life, including dating, so I sat him down for a conversation. I wanted to make sure we were clear about how we were moving forward with our relationship so we were both choosing to honor our established friendship as well as one another. Jeffrey was eager to dive right into things, but I insisted that we not make any changes until our next get-together. This would give us the opportunity to give it some more thought rather than doing anything rash that would change our friendship forever.

Soon after, we started a romantic relationship, but I abruptly put it to a halt just two weeks later. As I was waking up one morning, I received a powerful and disturbing message from my spirit guides. Like a movie playing right before my eyes, I was shown a string of images as well as the meaning of the images. First, I saw a replay of myself receiving the recent energy healing session from Jeffrey. I was face down on the treatment table, completely relaxed and unaware of what was really happening. Meanwhile, Jeffrey was standing next to the treatment table with his hand outstretched, intentionally placing an energy cord there in my root chakra. As I was shown these images, my guides explained to me that Jeffrey had then used that energy cord to send me strong sexual urges in order to manipulate me to sleep with him! I was so shocked to realize he had been energetically manipulating me! My guides then showed me that Jeffrey was secretly sexually involved with at least one other woman. Then my guides showed me multiple images of him placing his hands on many different women during his energy healing sessions in order to attach energy cords to each one. I was told that through these energy cords, his goal was to drain life force energy from each one of them, as well as to send them powerful "thought forms" and sexual urges in order to manipulate them into having sex with him.

The information had come through so clearly and I had no doubt as to the authenticity and accuracy. I was mortified about what I now knew, so I cancelled our plans for that week while I figured out how I wanted to proceed. I was so shocked to learn that my friend of three years was doing this to people, let alone me!

The following week, I arranged to meet him at my house for a very serious conversation. I told him what my spirit guides had shown me. I sternly emphasized, from one Reiki Master to another, that it is of vital importance that he immediately stop sourcing energy inappropriately from women, and that as an energy healer and Reiki Master, he absolutely should not be abusing his position of power like this. I told him I had been shown that he was involved with other women behind my back, and he responded, "Wow, you could see that? I'm impressed."

Clearly, he did not understand the importance of what I was telling him. I explained to him that effective immediately I would no longer be romantically involved with him, and I went into further detail about healthy and ethical ways a person should manage their energy without feeding off of, or manipulating others. I had already seen, through the previous women's healing circle, how harmful abuse of power can be between client and practitioner, and I felt I would have been horribly remiss if I did not explain things as clearly as possible to Jeffrey. Throughout our discussion, I was serious and straightforward, but I also tried to be kind and give him the benefit of the doubt. As we finished our meeting, he gave me a big hug, and then he came onto me again! At that point I got really frustrated and lost my patience. I felt he totally did not understand anything we had talked about!

We got together as friends a few more times over the next couple of weeks, but he continued to consistently hit on me despite my clearly set boundaries. I really had hoped we could go back to being just friends, but when it became clear to me he had no intention of honoring my personal boundaries, I told him not to contact me again.

About a year later I was attending a spiritual event with my friend, Raina. We were walking out of the building when we saw Jeffrey leaving with a woman I did not know. I took one look at Jeffrey and my jaw dropped open when I saw his energy.

"Oh my God, Raina, he's still doing it! I can see his energy, and he's even *worse* than before!" I turned to Raina, "You see him a lot at these events. Have you noticed that he places his hands on lots of women?"

Raina replied, "Oh yes! He is constantly giving shoulder and neck rubs, and it's always to the young, attractive women, *never* to any of the men or older women. I always thought that was a bit odd."

Raina can't see energy the way I do, so I pointed some things out to her. "Do you see how he is interacting with that woman? She clearly looks up to him and is following his lead. I can see by their energy that he's already hooked into her energetically. She doesn't realize she is under his control."

Raina replied, "He told me they were going to go to his place and do an energy healing session."

"Exactly. That's the primary way he taps into her energy. And do you see all that energy of sneakiness and secrets around him? Yet, he has really fine-tuned his 'ultra-spiritual guy' act over the last year to hide what he is really doing. Raina, didn't you say he is in a monogamous relationship with a girlfriend? But this is not her, correct?"

"Yep," Raina replied. "But whenever she's not around, he always leaves with a different woman."

I clarified, "Okay, well, if he is having affairs, yes, that lacks integrity and character, but it's none of our business. What really freaks me out is how he is knowingly manipulating people's energy. And he knows better! I know he knows better because I told him, point blank. I can't believe he's still doing it, and even worse than before!"

It was disconcerting to see a fellow energy healer intentionally and knowingly manipulating the energy of others, and yet, I had already done what I could by talking with him about it. After Raina and I saw him at that event, I began running into him occasionally at various community events, and I kept him at an awkward arm's length. After one particular event near my home, we chatted for a bit, and I invited him to my house for a cup of tea to clear the air. As we sipped tea in my living room, we both agreed that we would be running into each other more often and that we didn't want things to be so awkward. We agreed to be friendly to one another at community events and put the past in the past. I did attempt to broach the topic of his tendency to manipulate the energy of women, but when it became clear he was still completely denying the issue, I dropped the subject.

A few months later, something truly fascinating happened, and I don't think I would have seen the situation so clearly without having the past history and knowledge I had about Jeffrey. Raina and I were at another community spiritual event where Jeffrey was in attendance. Raina was sitting to my right with her boyfriend. Jeffrey went over to her and told her something. She smiled and nodded. Then, he came over to me, and rather than standing in front of me like he had with Raina, he came right up to my ear and placed his hand lightly on my shoulder.

In a low voice, he said, "I just wanted to let you know I'm going to be leaving now."

"Okay," I nodded. Then as he turned away, his hand that had been on my shoulder caressed down my arm as he turned completely and walked away. I was suddenly filled with a rush of sexual attraction for him.

About three seconds later, I realized what had happened. That S.O.B. had just re-attached an energy cord to me! Even after I had told him not to! "Oh, hell no! You're not allowed to have access to me!" I yelled in my mind, as I focused on energetically severing the cord he had just attached. I was totally floored by the gall this person had, and also fascinated by what I was discovering firsthand about energy attachments from sexual predators. One thing was for certain: I did not want anything to do with anyone who manipulates people's energy like that, and I most especially did not want anything to do with *him*.

After that, I kept Jeffrey at arm's length and never allowed him to touch me — no hand on the shoulder, no pat on the back, no hug, no handshake, no physical contact whatsoever. And I most certainly never allowed him to perform any type of energy work on me. I gave serious consideration to warning the community about him, but my past experience had taught me that the severe backlash for doing so would not be worth it. Speaking up usually caused people to support the perpetrator even more, rather than help fix the issue. So, I kept the information private between myself and a couple of close friends. Despite my best efforts to steer clear of this issue, here it was rearing its ugly head again.

The Phone Call

"So, what do you think, Maya?" Anne asked. "Jennifer said she saw a demon superimposed over Jeffrey's face when she was receiving a session from him at my open house. Do you think Jeffrey is being controlled by a demon?"

I answered carefully, intending to only speak my own truth and not answer for anything I had not experienced firsthand. "I have had some negative experiences with him in the past but as of yet I have not seen any demonic entities with him. I can't speak for Jennifer's experiences, but it certainly is possible. I really can't give you a definitive answer on what she experienced."

I felt comfortable with Anne, so I decided to share with her the personal details of my past situations with Jeffrey, including my firsthand experience with him plugging manipulating energy cords into me, as well as my observation of him as an energetic sexual predator. I lamented to her about how I felt terrible that he was still doing this to women, despite the fact that I had tried to intervene by telling him to stop. I felt guilty that my intervention had not worked and that he was even worse than before.

Anne was very kind in her response. "Maya, you really tried. You clearly explained to him what he was doing and that he should stop. If he chose to ignore you, that's on him. He's been clearly told what he's doing, so he can't claim the excuse that he doesn't realize what's happening. At this point, you can see that he's knowingly choosing to manipulate the energy of other people. It's clear that he's doing it intentionally."

I chatted with her about what had happened with the women's healing circle I had assisted with in the past, and how when I tried to speak out to the community, it caused a lot of outright denial, misled support of the perpetrators, and backlash to the people who had tried to speak up. Based on my past experiences, I felt that anything I did to speak up about Jeffrey would have negative results. I also explained to her that since Jeffrey and I had been romantically involved in the past, albeit briefly, anything I would say about him would likely be written off. I told her that I support a community intervention for Jeffrey, but that I choose to not have any further involvement with the issue. I still had hope that perhaps somehow Jeffrey would be receptive if other people (not me) approached him. Obviously, he had not taken me seriously, but perhaps if a group of people were to approach him about it, he might choose to stop his harmful behavior.

I told Anne, "I hope the information I've shared with you helps you discern whatever is best for your healing center. Everything I've shared with you is completely confidential, so I hope you'll keep it all in confidence. As for me, I really can't have any further involvement, so I won't be attending the upcoming community meeting where you'll be discussing the issue about Jeffrey."

"Yes, of course," she replied. "Thank you for opening up and sharing so much!"

We ended the call on a positive note, and I assumed I was done with the issue.

The following week, I got a very troubling email from Anne. She said that the community meeting had fallen through because everyone could not get their schedules to line up. She had met with Jeffrey privately and had a very heartfelt, honest conversation with him. Based on his response, she said she now feels he is very sincere in his positive convictions, and that any concerns I have are most likely based on hurt feelings I have from our past broken relationship. She said that in her assessment of the situation, she has decided to hire him as one of the featured energy healers for her healing center.

I took one look at her email and thought, "Oh God, he's hooked into her. She fell for it, even though I warned her."

I replied to her email in a professional manner, explaining that I respect her decision, but I do not agree. "Of course, you do have the right to do whatever you deem appropriate at your healing center. However, based on what I am seeing energetically, I still will not permit Jeffrey to perform any energy work on me, and I also will not bring any of my own students to any events in which he is a featured healer. This is for their own protection, as I would never knowingly invite them to participate in energies I believe are detrimental to them."

I explained to her that Jeffrey was just telling her what she wanted to hear, because I had observed this behavior in him many times. Part of his deceit is to deny everything and act genuinely concerned. I told her I wished her all the best and I was glad we were able to speak so openly and honestly with one another.

The next week I attended a chanting kirtan where Jeffrey was in attendance with his new romantic interest, Amber. After the concert was over, Jeffrey came over to chat with me one-on-one. He was telling me about some of his experiences from the prior week. He started laughing as he explained how he had been told that some women thought he had a demon working with him. He chuckled, "Even Anne gave me a talking to. I don't know what that was all about but I didn't take it seriously."

My mouth was agape. I took a breath and said, "I see." I wanted to talk to him right then and there, telling him that he should not be laughing! I was about to explain to him that perhaps people were concerned for a *reason*, that it is important that he stop laughing it off, that he should finally take responsibility for managing his energy *ethically*. Unfortunately, our conversation was interrupted before I could begin because someone came over to ask me a question. When I was finally freed up, Jeffrey and Amber were leaving. I felt utterly disappointed in Jeffrey for his response. I was beginning to see that no matter how many well-meaning people pointed this energy issue out to him, it was not doing a bit of good. He knew full well that he could continue his unethical behavior if he just stayed in denial and continued his act of the 'ultra-spiritual guy.' I could clearly see that he was still plugging in and sourcing energy off of women. As a leader in the spiritual community, it was disheartening to see this predatory behavior evolving in yet another energy healer.

I thought about Anne and how she, like others, was being duped. I totally understood why she believed him and had disregarded my warnings. He is very convincing, and a reasonable person might think I was just a jilted ex-lover who was seeing things from a distorted perspective. At that point, I took no further action, understanding how unlikely it was that people would believe me. But the truth of the matter is that I see the situation with crystal clarity. I have a very unique first-hand perspective in which I was clearly shown how he plugs energy cords into others.

With the acknowledgment that I had not wanted to be entangled in the issue in the first place, I withdrew my involvement and prayed for the best for all involved.

LESSON 3 – ALL ABOUT ENERGY CORDS

An energy cord is an "invisible" conduit which energetically connects one person to another. Energy can flow to or from a person through an energy cord, or even go both directions. Some energy cords are beneficial, such as with a mother or father connected in love to their infant child, or a loving, supportive connection between romantic partners or friends. Other energy cords are non-beneficial, such as with a controlling mother with her adult child, a manipulative co-worker, or a friend who drains your energy.

Energy cords come in all different shapes and sizes. Minor energy cords can be as thin as a thread. Others can look like spaghetti noodles. Moderate energy cords can look like an electrical cord, a water hose, or even tentacles. Larger energy cords can be as big as a fire hose, or even be composed of multiple smaller cords tangled together. I have even seen intricate webs of interlaced spaghetti-like cords.

In addition, some very old cords can be attached for lifetimes or even longer, while some may have been newly attached. The older the cord, the harder it may be to remove, while newly attached cords can usually be removed quite easily.

Most negative energy cords are attached unintentionally by people who know very little about energy; nevertheless, their emotions, thoughts, and intentions create dysfunctional energy connections with others. On the other hand, some people intentionally attach negative energy cords to others. These people have an awareness of energy and how to manipulate it to serve their own purposes. In some cases, energy cords can even be cloaked so they are nearly impossible to see even by the most adept clairvoyant. Practitioners of the dark arts can intentionally create cloaked energy cords that can last lifetimes for the unsuspecting victim. Even to the adept clairvoyant, these cloaked energy cords can appear completely clear and be almost impossible to locate.

How Negative Energy Cords Are Used

Keeping in mind that often there can be multiple energy cords going back and forth between two people, we are going to simplify things a bit by focusing on a scenario where there is just one cord. Let's say that Person A is the one who hooks a negative energy cord into Person B. Whether the cord is placed intentionally or unintentionally, the cord still works the same. Person A can either receive energy from, or send energy to, Person B, or they can do both. When Person A receives energy from Person B, they are literally sucking Person B's life force energy from them. In this type of relationship, we call Person A an 'energy vampire' or 'psychic vampire' because, much like an actual vampire that sucks blood, this person sucks energy from others.

How do you identify if you have an energy vampire in your life? Simple. If you feel inexplicably exhausted and depressed after you have had contact with this person, they almost certainly have at least one negative energy cord hooked into you. Remember that many people are unaware that they are doing this. Some people plug energy cords into others because on some level they learned this dysfunctional unconscious behavior along the way. Other people who source energy off of others may do so because they are depleted due to illness or ongoing fatigue. Yet, there are others who suck energy from others knowingly and deliberately, as in my previous story about Jeffrey.

Just as people can suck energy from others through energy cords, they can also send negative energy, dark thoughts, negative emotions, and manipulative intent. Let's use the example of Person A and Person B again, where Person A has hooked a negative energy cord into Person B. If Person A is feeling jealousy or anger toward Person B, all of those negative emotions are feeding right into Person B through that energy cord. Any dark thoughts Person A is having will be feeding into that energy cord as well, having a negative impact on Person B. And if Person A is a manipulator, they can knowingly or unknowingly send thoughts, intentions, and emotions in order to bend the person to their will.

I was so shocked when I was shown this through first-hand experience. When a manipulative person hooks into your energy, they can send you many types of messages to push you to do what they want! Here's an example: Person A is sexually attracted to Person B and wants to manipulate Person B into a sexual encounter. Person A sends powerful energy of sexual urges and strong lustful emotions to Person B. Person B suddenly begins feeling overpowering sexual attraction and obsessive thoughts about Person A. Person B erroneously thinks that these feelings are *their own*, when actually the feelings are being sent from Person A in order to manipulate Person B. Under this influence, Person B might choose to engage in a sexual relationship with Person A, not having any understanding of how they are being manipulated! In reality, Person B's thoughts and urges are not their own. Later, Person B blames themselves for getting into that situation, thinking it was their fault for saying 'yes,' and not having any understanding that Person A was actually running the show. This energetic scenario could occur out in the general dating world with someone who is a bit of a 'player.' On the more extreme end, this is how sexual predators are able to so easily manipulate their targets.

Here is an example: Have you ever been in a sexual relationship with someone you *knew* was bad for you, but you just could not get away? And even after you chose to leave, with 100% surety that you did *not* want to be with that person, you just could not get the person out of your mind? This was likely caused by not just one, but a web of energy cords still attached to you from that person. This is one of the reasons why I always recommend people go to an energy healer for a complete energy clearing after they have gone through a breakup. Get rid of those unhealthy energy cords so you can move on with your life.

In the scenario above, I have used sexual manipulation as the example, but energetic coercion through energy cords can involve any type of manipulation. A meddling family member, a controlling friend, a competitive co-worker, a scam artist...All of these scenarios, and more, can encompass the presence of negative manipulating energy cords.

How do you identify if someone is sending you negative or manipulating energy via energy cords? Make sure you are grounded and centered so you can be aware of your own thoughts, feelings, and emotions. When you are self-aware, you will more easily notice when foreign thoughts, energies, or intentions are attempting to influence you. Whenever you notice something that is questionable or out of the ordinary, do this simple yet powerful practice. Stop, take one or more deep breaths, drop your awareness down into your body, and ask yourself, "Is this (thought, feeling, emotion, etc.) mine?" If you get a sense that it is *not* yours, take another deep breath and evaluate who or what you may be receiving this energy from. Even if you are not sure, it will still prompt you to proceed carefully when you have an awareness of how negative energy cords could be influencing you.

One red flag for this type of energy cord is when you are suddenly overcome with feelings, thoughts, or intentions that are out of the ordinary for you. What gets tricky is the fact that sometimes energy predators work with your weaknesses, with those negative thoughts and feelings of your own that you have struggled with for a long time. Essentially, the thoughts and feelings are yours but the negative energy cord connection serves to magnify those energies. An example would be someone who has struggled with low self-esteem for a long time, and when someone hooks negative energy cords into them, the volume of the negative low self-esteem thoughts in their head gets turned *way* up.

Negative Energy Cords from Spiritual Beings

So far, I have discussed energy cords connected from one person to another. Energy cords can also be connected to or from groups of people, objects, locations, situations, and yes, even ghosts and all sorts of spiritual beings. Let's dive a little deeper into energy cords between a spiritual being and a person.

Everything that I have described about the energy cord dynamics between Person A and Person B would also apply to the dynamics between a spiritual being and a person. For example, a spiritual being (ghost, evil spirit, or other) can plug an energy cord into a person and source energy from that individual, essentially acting as an energy vampire. It is quite common for spiritual beings not connected with Divine Source to do this. Spirit energies, from human ghosts who have not moved on to Heaven, to evil spirits including all types from mischievous ghosts to the darkest demonic entities, love to feed off of human energy. In short, each of these are plugging into people to obtain life force energy rather than sourcing their energy from God. Even seemingly friendly ghosts often do this unintentionally.

For this reason, if you have a friendly ghost in your

home, it is best to ask them to move into the light to be with the Divine rather than sourcing energy off the inhabitants of your home. Evil spirits of all types love to feed off of humans. If there is an evil spirit in your home, or you suspect there is one attached to you, it is imperative you get it removed as soon as possible. If left unchecked, this type of energy cord can lead to serious issues, including illness and even death.

Spiritual beings can also manipulate people through energy cords—plugging into humans to feed them thoughts, feelings, and urges that initiate fear, drama, separation, and suffering. A ghost who was an addict in their physical human life will often seek out a vulnerable living human, plug into them, and encourage them to take part in addictive behavior so the ghost can act out their addiction vicariously through the human.

In addition, dark entities of all kinds plug into unsuspecting humans, doing everything they can to send the person dark, depressing, disturbing thoughts, encouraging harmful behavior toward self or others, causing mental illness, addiction, and physical illness. Why? They do this in order to activate human suffering and fear so they can feed off of the darkness they have initiated.

Spiritual Teachers and Energy Cords from Evil Entities

One alarming aspect of entity energy cords is how they are plugged into unwitting spiritual teachers and energy healers (not to mention other people in helping fields, like therapists, clergy, political leaders, and more). Here is how it works: The evil spiritual being plugs directly into the teacher/healer in order to obtain energetic access to all that person's clients and students. In your mind's eye, imagine a dark figure with an energy cord attached to the spiritual healer/teacher, and then multiple cords from the healer/teacher to each one of their clients.

In some scenarios, the entity is connected, via the healer/teacher, to hundreds and sometimes thousands of people! The clients and students are seeking spiritual guidance and healing, and yet if they are unlucky enough to connect with the wrong person, they will end up a victim of entity attachment. Now they are not only a victim themselves, but they are also part of a complicated web of dark energy involving their healer/teacher and all the other victims as well. As with all energy cords, the dark being can suck life force energy from the victims and can also send manipulating thoughts and harmful energy.

How does this even happen? Shouldn't a spiritual teacher/healer know better? Usually the teacher/healer is targeted for entity attachment for one or more of the following reasons: They do not use proper discernment in their spiritual work, calling in all sorts of spiritual beings without taking appropriate measures to ensure they are working only with beneficial beings. Without proper discernment, these teachers and healers end up gullibly working with evil entities that are pretending to be ascended masters or other high vibration beings. Some are targeted simply because they do not believe that evil entities exist. They ascribe to the popular belief that everything is from God, everything is light, and any expression of the dark is simply an illusion or projection. Those who do not believe in dark entities are the absolute easiest targets since they are completely blind to what is right under their nose.

How can you tell if you have an energy cord attached via an energy healer or spiritual teacher? This can be very tricky because by nature this type of scenario involves a whole lot of illusion. Energetically speaking, the healer/teacher may look very bright and shiny to potential followers. They may appear as a super-spiritual, highly evolved, beaming beacon of spiritual wisdom and healing. The person may have many followers who love them and rave about them, and their events and offerings may be well-attended. Some are even world-renowned. Yet, under the smokescreen of illusion is a whole lot of darkness. Some have no idea they are working with the dark, because they, too, are fooled by the illusion. Others are fully aware and do so knowingly and willingly for their own gain.

The dark absolutely delights in plugging into and working through spiritual healers and teachers. It is one of the most effective ways 'Team Dark' can gain access to many vulnerable spiritual seekers. Dark entities will feed negative energy and suck life force energy from the students and clients, lowering each person's vibration and life force, thus working to pull each person off their true high vibration soul's purpose. In addition, each person will be confused and distracted by the false teachings coming through their dark-directed spiritual teacher, each student believing that they are receiving actual truths when in fact the Dark Forces are intentionally directing each person off course from their divine mission.

When I became aware of this in my own community, and the world at large, I was completely shocked, and the truth was a heavy burden to carry. I saw how the dark was so often disguised as light, and unknowing, unprotected people were flocking to the false light in droves. It broke my heart and concerned me greatly. But I knew that speaking out about those under dark influence would only cause denial and resistance. Instead, I embarked on a mission to teach these truths to my own students both locally and online worldwide. I believe that having an awareness about this information can help greatly with one's ability to identify false light from true light.

For me, whenever I am thinking about attending any type of spiritual event, class, workshop, or healing session, I tune in intuitively regarding the healer, teacher, event, location, etc. to discern whether the energies are beneficial for me. If the situation is not beneficial, I notice one of two things. Either I (clairvoyantly) see dark entities attached via energy cords to the teacher, healer, or facilitator, and also connected into a web to those who were followers. And/or I (clairvoyantly) see false light. I see what looks like white light, except it is overly bright to the point where it hurts my eyes. I experience TRUE light as lovely and uplifting, and false light is blindingly bright, almost as though it is trying to overcompensate by making itself ultra-bright and alluring. Those who do not know any better are attracted to false light like moths to a flame.

If you want to avoid getting hooked into a web of dark energy cords, discernment is the number one key. Always listen to your own gut feelings. If something does not seem right, listen. Don't question your inner knowing, even if the person you are inquiring about has thousands and thousands of followers and is the most popular spiritual teacher or healer in the world. Even if you are not sure if the person is working with the Dark Forces, you can be certain that if something intuitively does not feel right, it simply is not going to be a good fit for you.

How to Get Rid of Negative Energy Cords

If you suspect you are the victim of an energy vampire, you can seek out an energy healer who knows how to cut energy cords. Some are trained only in how to channel healing energy (which is an important skill in and of itself) but they do not know how to remove non-beneficial energy. So, when contacting your potential energy healer, ask questions, find out if they know how to cut energy cords, and also be sure to ascertain if they are working with the integrity of energy that you wish to work with. A skilled, high-vibration healer can usually help you with clearing and healing far beyond what you would be able to do on your own.

With the proper knowledge, you do have the capacity

to cut cords and clear your energy without the help of an energy healer. You can create a very powerful and effective experience by working with your guardian angels, the archangels, and any other true high-vibration spiritual masters you wish to work with.

Cord Cutting Exercise

Sit comfortably in a quiet, peaceful place where you will not be disturbed. Begin by taking three slow deep breaths inhaling through your nose and exhaling through your mouth. As you continue to focus on your breath, allow your awareness to drop down into your body. Become aware of any areas of your physical body or aura where you sense there may be energy cord attachments. Do not worry if you have trouble tuning into any possible cords because you will still be able to do the cord cutting either way.

Before proceeding, you will need to ground and center. Take a moment to connect in with earth energy, allowing nurturing, grounding earth energy to flow up into your body through your feet and root chakra (energy center at the base of your spine). This will help you to feel safe, centered, and grounded through this process. Then, connect with your spiritual source, whatever that is for you (God, Goddess, Creator, source energy, etc.). Now call in your spiritual protection team. They may consist of any high vibration spiritual beings. I suggest working with Archangel Michael, who is the powerful protection angel, and who fights demons and other dark beings, working in tandem with Archangel Raphael, the healing angel. As you focus on your breath, ask Archangel Michael to come in with his sword of sapphire blue light to gently, yet effectively, cut all negative energy cords. Ask Archangel Raphael to send his green healing light into any areas where energy cords have been removed. This ensures that your energy field does not continue to have damaged areas which would make you vulnerable to future attack. Ask Archangel Michael to fill your whole being with his sapphire blue light of protection. Take a deep breath. Say "Thank you," and know that your energy is now free and clear of any energy cords you were ready to release.

You can repeat this process as often as you wish. If this is your first time doing a cord cutting the process may be a little intense as you release many long-standing energy cords. Be gentle with yourself. Allow extra time for rest, reflection, and self-care. Drinking a glass of water and getting extra sleep are the top two most effective tools for dealing with energetic detox.

CHAPTER 4 – PSYCHIC ATTACKS AND BOUNDARY VIOLATIONS

It was a sunny Saturday in late April when I decided to attend a public spiritual event about ten minutes from my home. As I scrolled down my Facebook feed, I saw a lovely event featuring a woman named Darlene, who channels messages from the angels. I walked into the local spiritual center with my heart open and in eager anticipation. When the class began, Darlene shared some of her personal angel stories and then began answering questions from individuals in the audience.

When it was my turn, I asked some questions about some health challenges I had had throughout my entire life. The angels (through Darlene) shared that the reason I was so physically and energetically sensitive was because, as I child, I was not celebrated, and as a survival mechanism, I learned to draw other people's suffering into me. The angels said that this has caused all sorts of issues for my body. I told the angels (Darlene) all about what I do on a daily basis to clear my energy and set up grids of protection. They said those things are all good, but it is not enough, that what is occurring between my energy and the energy of others is totally subconscious, so none of the conscious things I was doing would actually fix that. I found the messages quite fascinating and I knew that I had a lot to ponder.

During the break, I chatted with Darlene. I felt a sisterly affinity with her from the moment we met. She gave me a big hug and we immediately dropped into a deep discussion about how important it is for healers to actively engage in their own healing work on themselves.

"When healers don't work on their stuff," Darlene said, "they end up energetically attaching to their clients and causing them harm."

This immediately sparked my interest. "I couldn't agree more!" I exclaimed. So many in the spiritual community seemed to be oblivious or in denial about this issue, and Darlene actually *got* it! I was eager to learn more about her perspectives, so I arranged a private angel healing session with her.

"Darlene," I told her, "I'm very discerning who I will let work on me these days. I'm so excited to find a colleague on a similar wavelength!" We each pulled out our phones and scheduled my session for two weeks in the future.

After the class, I went home and sat in my backyard to enjoy the sunshine. With my bare feet on the grass, I grounded the energies I had received at that afternoon's angel channeling event. I sent out a prayer of gratitude for the day and for having the opportunity to connect with Darlene.

As I allowed my mind to relax into a gentle awareness, I began to ponder some of my decisions regarding Anne and her healing center. She had invited me to host some of my upcoming events at the center, but now I was feeling unsure. I am not someone who boycotts others, because I believe that is an unethical, unkind, and unnecessary thing to do. I did however feel very uncomfortable bringing my students to her center. In a general sense, it was not a match for me or my students. More specifically, I would have been out of integrity with my students if I knowingly sponsored my event where a known energetic sexual predator was on site. I truly wanted to support Anne and her new healing center, but I just could not, in good conscience, hold my events there.

A few days later when I felt fully grounded in my decision, I sent Anne an email, thanking her for inviting me to teach at her center, and explaining why I would not be able to. A week later she sent me a very odd reply. She said that she had received intuitive information about me that she needed to share with me. I was horrified to read paragraphs about my deepest, most personal innermost struggles, information that I had *never* shared with her, all of which she had accessed intuitively without my permission. I felt violated and angry that she had done this. My gut immediately knew she had done this as an ego-based 'power play,' to prove to me how powerful she is. She did not like the boundaries I had set regarding her healing center, and she felt the need to show me that she knows my vulnerabilities. Admittedly, I had not seen her power play coming because I had felt such a connection to her in the past. Plus, I have the habit of assuming other people have the same level of integrity I do. Sometimes that assumption causes me to be blindsided!

I wanted to nip this boundary violation in the bud. I immediately replied to her email, stating that she had accessed my energy and my personal information without my permission, and this is a blatant boundary violation. I told her in no uncertain terms that she was not allowed to violate my boundaries again.

The next day, she sent a long reply, explaining that as a practicing witch, she has a special gift from God, and when she receives messages, she shares them. She explained that her responsibility is to simply share these messages, and it is not her job to hold the hand of the person receiving it to ensure they receive it gently. I read the message a couple of times, my mouth agape. It was the most condescending email I had ever received.

I am the type of person who tries to gain perspective on what is *really* going on behind any type of personal drama. It is just so easy to get sucked into our own emotional responses. I took a few deep breaths, then contacted a couple of friends to ask their opinion. This started an interesting and important conversation about the ethics of accessing the energy and information of other people without their permission. Yes, some people do it, but no, it is not ethical. The thing is, some people who are psychically open do inadvertently receive information about others without even trying. In those instances, it is up to the psychic to remain in integrity, to keep the information to themselves, and not share it with others. Unfortunately, there are some who share unsolicited psychic information as a means to inflate their ego and sense of personal power.

You have probably had someone give you unsolicited advice in the past that you could feel was not about helping you, but indeed was all about the other person's intent to make you feel small. Unsolicited psychic advice works much the same way. Imagine that someone breaks into your house and reads your private journal without your consent. Then, they call you or send an email, mentioning all the deeply personal things they read about in your journal along with their own opinions about all of it. Most people would be mortified! It can be quite unsettling when someone accesses your personal information without your consent.

Later that day, I was sitting under a tree in my backyard writing in my journal. Suddenly I noticed a crow in the branches above my head. It was making an awful squawking racket and with its head turned, it was glaring right at me with one piercing black eye. A chill went down my spine, and I suddenly thought of Anne, that somehow, she was watching me through the crow. That thought seemed too peculiar, so I pushed it out of my mind and tried to ignore the bird. Every time I went outside, the crow was always there, either in the tree or perched on the eaves of the shed, glaring and squawking at me. I have always loved birds, and I had never had a crow act that way with me before. Although it was odd, I did not assume it was anything more than strange animal behavior.

I was noticing more and more that there was an

unusually high amount of drama energy coming into my life. Over the years, I had carefully cultivated a peaceful, grounded lifestyle, so the big upswing in drama was quite noticeable and a little unsettling. What I recognized was that it was *other* people trying to pull me into *their* drama, and I did not like that one bit! Most of the stuff they were trying to pull me into had absolutely nothing to do with me, and I felt annoyed that despite my best efforts, I kept getting sucked in. I decided it was time for some significant boundary setting on an energetic level.

I went out into my backyard, sat down on the grass, and went into prayer. I asked my angels and guides to set up an impenetrable wall that would completely block the energy of any people or situations that were not beneficial for me, that they would not be able to see or access my energy whatsoever, that they would not be able to send, receive, or attach energy or intent to me in any way whatsoever. I then thought of some specific people and wrote their names down in my journal, along with my prayer, so my intent would be crystal clear. I asked that God, my angels, and my spirit guides hold me in the light, always and in all ways. I asked that they make me invisible to those who have ill intent, and to make me magnetic and fully visible to those who are a positive match for me, and that the most benevolent people and energies surround me always.

I sat in prayer and picked a couple of oracle cards from one of my angel decks. The first was the Archangel Michael card, and the message was, "I am protecting you against lower energies, and guarding you, your loved ones, and your home." I also picked cards that indicated that I am a leader and counselor and that at this time I needed to focus on healthy lifestyle habits. The messages were reassuring and comforting.

I pondered why there had been so much unnecessary drama lately. Deep in prayer, I set a clear intention that it is no longer necessary for this pattern to continue. I asked for all chaos, drama, boundary violations, and dark energy to be cleared out now. I asked that the negative energies be replaced with light, love, harmony, peace, grounded-ness, clear insight, energetic strength, wisdom, integrity, centeredness, health, vitality, delight, joy, light-heartedness, fun, playfulness, sweetness, pleasure, and God's grace. I said thank you and trusted that now that I had set clear boundaries and intentions, things would return to normal peace.

A couple of nights later, I had horrible nightmares and woke with feelings of dread. Wondering what might be going on, I called my friend, Sandra.

"It sounds like a psychic attack to me." She was always good at nailing things right on the head. "I bet Jeffrey is sending you some negative energy."

"Hmm, could be," I responded. Being both open-minded and skeptical, I replied, "Either way, I should consider it."

Later that day, I contacted Elizabeth and Terri, two of the women who had been helping Anne set up her new healing center. I asked them if they were experiencing any unusual issues. Both responded back to me quickly, saying that they had been dealing with ongoing psychic attack from Jeffrey. Terri's health issues had suddenly and mysteriously grown much worse. In Elizabeth's case, the attack was affecting her loved ones. Her boyfriend had suddenly started having seizures (even though he had never had them before), and her dog had become inexplicably ill.

None of us were completely sure what was going on, but we all decided to take precautions just in case. I went through my house and found any objects that may have been connected with Jeffrey or Anne. I placed them in a Tupperware container, filled the container with water, placed the lid on top, drew Reiki symbols on top of the container, said a prayer for protection, and placed the container in the freezer in order to 'freeze' any energetic access they had to me via these objects. Right after that, I did a simple house clearing while walking from room to room burning sage and saying prayers of protection. I also affirmed that I would ask Darlene about this at my angel healing appointment the following Friday.

That evening I chatted with my friend, Sandra. She told me that this time I would *really* have to step up as a leader, as opposed to last time (with the women's healing circle) when I stepped up but then went into hiding when things got hard. She said that this time I would need to take more action. At that time, I felt I needed to gain more information on exactly what that action should be. I wanted to proceed with clarity and intention, but I was very nervous about the whole thing. Sandra encouraged me, saying that I am stronger than I think, and that the only reason I was being targeted for psychic attack was because I am powerful and those sending the attack know it and are threatened. Apparently, God was putting all of this in front of me for a reason and I was still discerning what that was!

Despite the dark cloud of psychic attack looming over my head, I focused my attention on preparing for the upcoming one-day women's retreat I would be facilitating. I had put on several women's retreats over the years, but I had taken a break from it for the last few years as I waited for the economy to improve and business to pick up. I was very excited that this retreat had sold out a week ahead and that there was so much interest! As I busily prepared, I created the plan for the day, organized volunteers, and packed up all the supplies. I drove to the retreat center the evening before to set up and get a good night's sleep.

The retreat was to be held at a lovely refurbished barn out in the country. When I arrived and got out of my car, I heard drumming in the distance. Knowing that my retreat participants would not be arriving until the next day, I figured it was another group enjoying the land. I stood and breathed in the fresh air and the distant drumming added to the magic of the moment. As I walked down the path toward the rhythms, I felt my heart expand and fill with gratitude for this special place. Turning the corner, I found a small group of women sitting around a little campfire, their faces painted with tribal markings, steadily beating their drums and singing goddess songs. I saw Donna, the proprietor of the land, and gave her a great big hug. The women asked if I would join them, but I declined. I was exhausted from getting ready for the retreat, and I still had some unpacking and prep work to do. I joined in for about five minutes of drumming then bowed out to finish my work and get some rest.

After getting everything set up for the next day's festivities, I climbed into the bed in the downstairs guest bedroom and fell fast asleep. In the middle of the night, I woke from a deep sleep. When I opened my eyes, I saw the apparition of a woman standing in the middle of the room looking directly at me. Her face was painted in a tribal pattern similar to the women who had been drumming around the campfire earlier that evening. I wondered why this particular ghost was present, one with tribal face paint. Perhaps it was because the campfire women had inadvertently called her in? I wasn't certain, but I knew I needed to be sure to clear the entire facility before the event started in the morning.

My volunteer crew arrived early to help me do some final set-up and energetically clear the space. The retreat turned out beautifully, even better than expected. We had nearly fifty amazing women gathered that day for drumming, dancing, sharing, healing, and feasting.

The next day, I was tired, but it was a good tired, the kind you feel after an important accomplishment. I was amazed at my own ability to hold energetic space for so many people as I took them through a deep transformation process. After years of longing to share my gifts with others, I was beyond grateful to be at a time in my life where students were ready to accept what I had to offer.

Following the retreat, I had long phone conversations with Terri and Elizabeth about the situations with Anne and Jeffrey. Both Terri and Elizabeth had withdrawn their involvement at the center, as they had previously been deeply engaged in its initial establishment and inner workings. Both were continuing to have indications of psychic attack being sent their way. I chatted with both, making suggestions on how they could reverse any possible attacks and protect themselves.

One thing we realized as we talked was that the boundary issues with Anne had been occurring long before the issues with Jeffrey had arisen. All three of us found that it was not uncommon for Anne to use a person's personal information as ammunition against them, betraying both privacy and trust. As I pondered recent events, I realized that I had misjudged Anne in the beginning. When we first met, I thought she had wonderful energy and that we were on a similar wavelength. But after my own recent experiences, and also understanding that she had also done this to others, I realized that I had trusted her too easily. In my habit of wanting to see the best in people, I had ignored blatant red flags.

As for Jeffrey and the larger issue of energy healing practitioners energetically feeding off of their clients, it had become abundantly clear to me that directly speaking to those involved to ask them to stop does *not* work. At that point, I felt that speaking directly to the perpetrators or those who support them only results in outright denial, actions to discredit those speaking up, and sometimes even outright psychic attack toward those trying to help. Trying to directly intervene was just stirring the pot and unnecessarily sucking away a lot of our energy

As I pondered more about the situation, I decided that I would just have to adopt the attitude that the predator issues are none of my business. We are all on different levels of our personal evolution. Yes, Jeffrey, and others, are outright harming people but there is nothing I can directly do about it. He and the others refuse to stop. It is *their* karmic shit storm, not mine. I feel that I did make true and honest efforts to help with the situation, but I now knew that it does no good. My job is to focus on what is in front of me, to teach my own students about ethics; the importance of doing their own personal development work (because if you don't, you can cause real harm to your clients); how to appropriately source energy (and not source it from your clients); how to know if someone has attached an energy cord to you; how to identify signs of a sexual predator; what is spiritual dysfunction; and more! I had been teaching these things to my students in my Leadership Training for Energy Healers courses, and now I felt it was time to teach it to the larger community on a more regular basis. Even if I could not take *direct* action to stop energetic predators and other unethical behavior in my community, I *could* make a difference by teaching my own students these important ethical concepts.

The past few weeks had involved much more drama than usual. I was more than ready to mark the end of it! I blessed everything that occurred and everyone involved, released it all with love, and welcomed peace back into my life. I was now completely clear about my role going forward—that I would focus on my own teaching, and release everything else.

LESSON 4 – THE ETHICS OF ENERGY

The question of when and how it is ethical to access other people's energy comes up quite often in my classes on Reiki, energy healing, and intuitive development. This topic also comes up quite often from people who are on the receiving end of unethical energy manipulation. When people ask about personal and professional boundaries, I know it is a very good sign because their default intent is to try to operate from a place of integrity. (Otherwise, they would not be interested in asking the question in the first place.) I am going to share with you my own code on this subject; however, it will be up to you to get clear about your own personal code of ethics. I know many people who have a much looser code of ethics than I do. Everyone is unique, and many people choose their code based more on their own self-interest rather than the interest of the whole. Even though I might not agree with every person's ethical code, I deeply respect the right for each person to choose their own path.

A good way to judge whether your actions are aligned with integrity is to ask yourself *honestly* if your actions are motivated by your own self-interest, personal gain, or ego, or if your actions are motivated by a truly loving intent to contribute for the highest and best good of all. Most of the time, when your intent is for the most benevolent outcome for all involved, you will be right on track ethically. It is human nature, and so easy, to tell ourselves the lie that our intentions are altruistic while we are actually in denial about our ego leading the show. This is why it is so important to be totally honest with yourself and to keep yourself in check. Ask yourself what is truly motivating you. The most important thing is that you stay true to your personal code, whatever that may be.

Permission to Send Healing Energy
First, let's talk about the ethics of sending healing energy to others. By healing energy, I am referring to Reiki, any type of energy healing practice, faith healing, prayer, etc. which can be performed either in person or at a distance. The most obvious approach is to ask the person permission. A simple question will suffice. "I'd like to pray for you. Would that be all right?" Or, "Do I have your permission to do some Reiki for you?" If they say, "Yes," then go ahead and proceed. If they say, "No," then accept their answer and don't try to force it.

Every person has free will, and it is never up to you to impose your own will onto another. Even if you can clearly see that your healing energy will bless them greatly, it is not up to you to decide what is best for them. Some people are uncomfortable receiving prayer or energy healing if it does not match with their personal, spiritual, or religious beliefs. Some people are simply uncomfortable with receiving anything at all from others. You must honor that. Some may not want to receive the healing you offer because they are emotionally attached to the negative situation in some way. And yet others may have a soul contract to have the experience of a personal challenge to bring about some type of learning or soul deepening. It is not up to you to figure out why they don't want to receive your well-intended healing gift, and it is not up to you to judge. Your job will be to simply trust that everyone is exactly where they need to be.

In my own case, I am very particular about whom I want working with my energy because I recognize that, despite the wonderful intentions of others, not everyone's vibrations are a good match for every individual on the planet. In fact, when someone of a lower vibration than you performs Reiki or energy healing, it can actually lower your vibration. In addition, if the person has any spirit attachments or other negative energy issues, they can inadvertently pass those issues onto you. Reiki itself is universal life force energy, and its essence brings healing to all people, no matter their vibration or level of spiritual evolution. However, in order to perform Reiki, the practitioner enters into the recipient's energy field, and by doing so, has an impact on the energy of the other person. This occurs because of something called 'entrainment.' When two different vibrations come together, they tend to level one another out. The lower vibration will raise a bit and the higher vibration will lower a bit so that they essentially meet in the middle. The exception is when someone of a higher vibration consciously holds their vibration high, therefore, raising up the person of the lower vibration. This occurs when a high vibration energy healer or spiritual teacher assists their students or clients in raising their vibrational level. Keep in mind, if the teacher or healer is of a lower vibration than their client, it will have either a neutral or detrimental effect on the recipient.

I will share a brief story to illustrate what an energy violation looks like. Several years ago, I was attending a local metaphysical fair as a customer. As I walked around the aisles of the fair, I chatted with different people. At one point, I rounded the corner and ran into a couple that I knew. He was a massage therapist and she was an assistant minister at a local church. We were in the middle of chatting about something when, all of a sudden, she stopped talking, declared that I had a block in one of my chakras, and announced that she needed to clear it for me. Without asking, she started waving her hand around and working with my energy. Back then, I did not have the healthy boundaries that I do today, and so, rather than speaking up, I simply stood there feeling pissed off.

Since that incident, there have been many times I have spoken up when people have invaded my energy without permission. In fact, even when people ask permission, I have often said, "No, thank you." I remember another time when I was walking through a metaphysical fair. I walked past a particular booth advertising spiritual healing, and the very nice man in the booth asked if he could do energy healing on me. I looked at him, smiled, and said, "No, thank you." He replied, "It's free. There's no cost." I repeated, "No, thank you." I noticed the hurt and confused expression on his face and knew he did not understand my reason for declining. I am certain that he was a gifted healer and had helped many clients. My gut told me that he was just not a good fit for me. I walked on, feeling good that I was making choices that were beneficial for my energy.

When You Are Unable to Ask Permission

What happens when you are unable to ask permission? Perhaps the person is unconscious or not in a clear mental state that would allow them to understand and give consent. Or perhaps, you do not even know the person, such as when you would like to send healing intent to people you hear about on the news or social media. What do you do then? Is it all right to proceed without permission?

There is a simple technique I recommend in these situations. Before you proceed with sending healing intent to the person, go into a gentle meditation, connect with the person's spirit or Higher Self, and ask the person "Is it alright if I send you Reiki/prayer/etc.?" You may receive the answer in a variety of ways. You may hear a 'yes' or 'no' in your mind (in your own voice or in their voice). You may feel your heart open and expand, or you may feel it close. You may sense a feeling of well-being in your body, or you may suddenly feel unwell. Refer back to Lesson 2 on Intuition for additional tips on receiving intuitive information. Generally speaking, if you feel expanded, uplifted, and well, the answer is 'yes,' and if you feel contracted or unwell, the answer is 'no.'

Once you receive your answer, you will know how to proceed. If you get a 'no,' then let it go and don't try to force it. You can always check again in a few days or weeks because the person may feel differently in the future. Any time you check, remember to do so without any expectation.

If you get a 'yes,' you can proceed by saying this prayer or intention. "I now send this Reiki/prayer/etc. for the highest good of [recipient] to receive and utilize it as they wish and for the highest good of all. Please allow any energy that is not wanted to be recycled into the Universe (or into the Earth)."

The Manipulation of Energy

In this chapter, I have discussed sending prayer and energy healing practices. Now let's discuss the manipulation of energy via magickal practices like spell work, rituals, bindings, hexes, curses, and etc. Magickal work itself is not bad if it is used with benevolent intent and for the highest good of all involved. Those that work with white magick to lovingly assist those around them are advised to follow the instructions above for obtaining consent. Even if your intent is loving and helpful, it is important to always ask for consent.

Many reading this will automatically know that it is highly unethical to send ill intent to someone through a hex or curse. However, there are a great many magickal practitioners who work in gray areas. In other words, their personal code tells them that they are justified in sending malevolent or manipulating energy if it benefits them personally. Perhaps someone annoyed or angered them, so they feel it is their right to seek revenge. Or perhaps they want to support their friend who just got dumped, so they will offer to put a curse on the ex. There are a million reasons why people choose to justify actions that are less than ethical.

Yes, the reality is that people do intentionally and knowingly cast curses and hexes. It is not just the stuff of Hollywood movies. It really does happen! I think it is important to point out that many high-integrity people in the world assume that others around them are also high-integrity. As such, they can get blindsided when they realize someone sent a hex or curse their way. Since they themselves would never dream of doing such a thing to anyone, it does not even cross their mind that someone would do it to them. If you fall into this noble yet vulnerable category of assuming the best of people, now your eyes are more open to the reality of what really does happen in our world. It is beneficial for you to understand that not all practitioners work with the highest intent.

Now, for those reading this that choose to work in gray areas, sometimes doing magickal work to benefit others, and sometimes to manipulate or cause harm to others for your own benefit, I suggest that you sit down with a journal or notebook and write out your own personal code of ethics. Everyone's code is unique to them. Whatever your code may be, remember to be crystal clear about what you are doing and why so you are always anchored in your own truth. The very worst thing you can do is to have gray ethics simply because you're on autopilot, you have never taken the time to think about your own personal code, or you are blindly following the example of your magickal peers or mentors. Become authentic and intentional about your own unique personal ethical code and be sure to follow it at all times.

Of course, my own truth (which I feel very strongly about!) is that it is never advised to send manipulating or malevolent energy to others, whether it is through magickal practice or any other means. Some people believe in The Law of Three — that anything you send out comes back to you threefold. Whether you believe in The Law of Three or not, it is simply a crappy thing to do bad things to people! My advice is that if you would not want someone to do it to you, don't do it to others.

It is important to remember that there are many people out there in the world who misuse power via unethical energy practices. As a personal example, many years ago, I was a member in a local women's group that included mentoring in business, intuition, and magickal practices. The facilitator of the group (let's call her Sue) was very transparent about the fact that she preferred to work in the gray, using both light and dark magick as it suited her. She also taught magickal practices for enhancing one's business. The material that was taught was interesting and seemed harmless enough, that is, until one day, my friend (who was also in the group) and I realized that energetic practices were being used to manipulate the members of the group, including us. We called each other to discuss what was going on and came to the conclusion that we had been keeping our heads in the sand, ignoring clear and obvious signs that Sue would behave in that way. She had been teaching magickal techniques for business, but when we assessed the material more closely, we realized that the techniques were all about energetically manipulating not only one's business, but also one's clients and potential clients. For example, methods were taught to psychically entice potential clients to sign up or to encourage current clients you didn't want to work with anymore to leave. When we looked honestly at this, it became clear to me that Sue had given me a great big, huge energetic shove out of her program. I tend to have a pretty strong energy, and not all facilitators are comfortable with this within their groups. I could feel that she was done with me and was eager to draw in some new students. Out with the old, in with the new. There is nothing wrong with wanting to fine tune your client base so it better fits your vision for your business. But, using magickal practices to make that happen (rather than talking with the person directly) is a misuse of power and against the free will of others. In short, it is blatantly unethical.

It is up to you to decide where you stand on this issue and to be crystal clear about your own code of ethics. Once you have established your own personal code, be sure to uphold others to your own standards. In other words, if you do not believe it is okay for you to manipulate the energy of others, you are likely also not okay with people doing that to you. It might be best to distance yourself from those who engage in that type of practice and any other practices that do not match your personal code. You are absolutely under no obligation to allow others to do things to you that you do not agree with. The clearer you are about your own ethical code, the clearer you will be in your discernment of the behavior of others around you, and what you will and will not allow in your life.

The Ethics of Receiving Intuitive Information

Everyone on the planet has intuitive abilities, some more than others depending on natural talent and extent of practice. Even a moderately psychic person can intuitively tune into a person or situation to gain a better understanding. We all do it, oftentimes without even thinking about it. You can probably recall times when you met someone and instantly knew you could or could not trust them, or when you had a bad feeling about something and decided to take a different course of action instead. These are all healthy uses of intuition.

Using one's intuition is a bit of a gray area when it comes to the privacy of others. When you tune in somewhat softly, you may just pick up surface information about the person. If you tune in deeply, you may be able to perceive very private details about a person. I liken this to the difference between meeting someone in person and making observations about them based on how they present themselves, compared to going into a person's house without their consent, rummaging through their personal items, and reading their diary.

Some people who have strong intuitive abilities will intentionally do the equivalent of reading another person's journal. It is a blatant violation of privacy to do this without the person's consent. Now, if the person has given consent, all is well, as in the case when a client hires a psychic to do a reading for them. A violation of consent would occur when someone goes to a massage therapist thinking they are just going to get their sore muscles worked on, and the massage therapist, who also happens to be quite intuitive, starts blathering private or personal information to the person receiving the massage. Another example of violation of privacy occurs when someone is going through their mundane life, like shopping at the grocery store, they intentionally or unintentionally receive information about another shopper, and proceed to share it with them without the recipient's consent. Have you ever received unsolicited advice from a stranger? While sometimes the advice may be welcomed, many others may feel that it is an intrusion. If in doubt, ask for permission.

Some who are very open psychically will accidentally receive intuitive information without even trying. There is no need to feel bad about this, as it even happens to people with the very best of intentions. If you accidentally receive intuitive information about a person that is of a private nature, it will be up to you to decide whether or not to share that information with the person. When in doubt, don't share. If you feel deeply compelled to share, you can ask for consent to share with the person. This allows the person to choose whether they want to receive the information or not, and honors their free will. I like saying something like, "I've just received some intuitive information for you about [situation]. Would you like me to share it with you?" When you say this to someone, you are showing respect for their right to choose. Do not take it personally if the person declines, because it is not up to you to choose what is best for them.

Even if a person gives consent, it will still be up to you to use your professional discernment to decide what should be shared and what you should just keep to yourself. The truth is, not everything is meant to be shared, and it is your responsibility as an intuitive being to respond with integrity when you receive information.

In my own personal code, I do often read 'surface' information about people as I go through my day so that I can knowledgably choose if the person is safe and trustworthy, if they have good intentions, etc., but I do not ever intentionally tune into people's personal information. In sharing information with others, I always ask for consent. I do not blurt out shocking or upsetting news like someone's partner is having an affair, or that they should dump their partner. If the person is a close personal friend, I might choose to share the information in a kind and gentle way if I truly feel called to do so. I also don't predict a person's death or horrible accidents in their future. Doing so initiates undue fear. Besides that, the future is always shifting and changing due to the free will actions of everyone involved. If anyone chooses to step out of their usual actions, they may indeed shift the entire trajectory of future events for their life and the people around them. Why give someone terrifying news, knowing full well that if they believe in what you tell them, they have the likelihood to create a self-fulfilling prophecy based on what you have said? In that way, you become partially responsible for what happens to them.

Now, I am not in any way saying you should always avoid sharing bad news with someone. I give people so-called bad news all the time when they come to me for psychic readings or energy healing sessions. Rather than frame it in the energy of doom and gloom, fear and urgency, I frame the news as a heads-up for the person, allowing them to take empowered action to encourage the best possible outcome.

One example was when a middle-aged couple sat down at my table when I was doing readings at a local psychic fair. The minute I looked at them together I immediately knew that he was having an affair, actually multiple affairs, and that she was getting walked all over by this guy. Part of me wanted to blurt out that she needed to dump this cheating dirt-bag, but I knew that would only serve to confuse the woman and put the man into defensive denial mode. So, I proceeded to shuffle my oracle cards, lay the cards out on the table, and begin sharing what I saw. The cards clearly showed that infidelity was taking place, and since the cards so obviously illustrated the relationship situation, the man looked at me suspiciously and announced that he was going to leave us and walk around the fair. After he left, I talked with the woman gently yet directly about the relationship patterns she had been repeating over and over again over the years, patterns in which she was giving her power away and not being truly cherished and honored by her partner. All in all, it was a very empowering reading for her, because I gave her many suggestions on how to take her power back in her relationships and her life. Now, if I had simply blurted out that her boyfriend was cheating on her, we would have missed out on the opportunity to talk about the real root of the issue.

The above example illustrates how I deal with sharing potentially volatile, upsetting, or frightening intuitive information. I am careful to always tell the truth with a focus on helping to empower the recipient. There are many intuitives out there who purposely say shocking or upsetting things to their clients as a means of making their clients dependent upon them. (The idea is that if the client is dependent, they will come back for more sessions and pay more money.) This is a deceptive business tactic used all too often, and I strongly recommend against it.

When You Curse Others
A friend asked me a very important question the other day. She wanted to know if a person can send malevolent energy to another person unintentionally — simply by telling them off. She went on to explain that when telemarketers call her, she goes on a tirade, not only spouting off obscenities, but also telling them she hopes they suffer a horrible death.

The answer is a resounding YES. You absolutely do send energetic harm to others when you wish horrible things upon them. Flipping people off in traffic, telling off that person who annoys you, hoping your business competitor fails, wanting your ex to suffer, or wishing a horrible death to a telemarketer or the employees at the DMV, these are all examples of sending harmful energy to real people.

I get it. No one likes calls from telemarketers, and some people in the world can just be downright annoying. But, we need to always be responsible for the energy we send out into the world, as well as the energy we direct toward others. We all get mad sometimes, especially when there is injustice involved. Just the other night, I was feeling pretty upset about a local business that had treated me badly and had been more interested in my money than in treating me like a real human being. Here's the thing. We are *all* responsible for the energy we send out, and if you are trained in working with energy, you are even more responsible. Those who have developed the skill of focusing their energy can end up causing real harm to someone (equivalent to doing an actual curse on them) if they let their anger or jealousy get the best of them.

When I catch myself experiencing powerful negative thoughts toward another person, I take a breath and say a prayer, asking that all of the emotions coming out of me be redirected so they do not cause any harm. I imagine the energy flowing down into the earth to be recycled, or I imagine the energy being carried away by angels. This allows me to process and release my emotions rather than stuffing it all inside, while also ensuring that the process is not causing harm to others.

Now, it should not even need to be said that it is unethical to knowingly and intentionally send malevolent energy to others. Whether it is through aware focused intent or by taking part in casting a hex or curse, it is just plain wrong. Don't do it.

Your Own Code

Now that you have more information about what it means to access another person's energy, it is time for you to get clear about your own code of ethics. It is not up to me to decide for you. You must decide for yourself. Take the time now to answer the following questions.

1. What are your personal guidelines when sending prayer, Reiki, energy healing, or healing intent to others? Are there any instances when you feel it is alright to send energy without explicit permission? If so, explain.

2. What is your personal code regarding the energetic manipulation of people or situations through magickal or other esoteric practices? Are there any instances where you feel it is alright to partake in such practices? Explain.

3. What are your personal guidelines about intentionally trying to access private information about others via intuitive means? Are there any instances when you feel it is alright to access someone's information without their permission? If so, explain.

4. What are your personal guidelines about sharing private intuitive information that you've come to

know unintentionally? In what instances would you share the information with the recipient, and in what instances would you choose not to share?

5. What are your personal guidelines about sharing potentially volatile or frightening intuitive information with someone? If you do share the information, what is your method of sharing?

6. When you feel negative emotions such as anger or jealousy toward another person, how will you deal with it?

CHAPTER 5 – A PUZZLING EMAIL

I sat down at my desk with my morning tea and turned on my computer. There was an email from Anne.

"Hi Maya. Jeffrey recently shared with me that there was a lot of gossip about him at your recent women's retreat, and that your event was quite the rumor mill! I don't want to be associated with a teacher who encourages gossip and unprofessional behavior at her events. I hope there are no hard feelings, but I just can't be involved with you any longer."

What on earth was going on? The retreat had been a lovely, beautiful event, filled with sisterhood and fun, and if I *had* observed any gossip, I certainly would have discouraged it. I knew full well that I had not encouraged gossip at my retreat, but Jeffrey was apparently spreading a whole different story. I knew exactly what he was doing because I had seen this type of gaslighting behavior before from predators of all types. He was trying to proactively discredit me just in case I tried to pull the veil off of his little energy predator operation. Even though I had made every effort to stay out of it, he was still spreading rumors in order to create a smokescreen and cover up what he was really doing. The best way to take the attention off of himself was to point the finger toward the person he saw as the biggest threat—me. He knew I had spoken out about the issue of sexual predators in the past, and he was likely nervous I was going to do it again. I was frustrated that he was spreading rumors about me, and I wanted no part in the drama he was trying to kick up. I truly wanted no involvement in any of it!

But, it was becoming evident that the problem was not going away on its own. I decided to nip this gossip in the bud by sending Jeffrey a text message and asking if we could have a conversation. I wanted to talk with him directly to resolve the situation once and for all. Within minutes, he replied to my text, saying he was unavailable to talk and that he was not involved with the rumor. Flat out denial and avoidance were two of his common manipulation tactics I had observed many times in the past. Since he was not willing to talk, I decided to let it go. Realistically, I knew there was no effective way to clear things up with a master manipulator such as Jeffrey.

I went ahead and replied to Anne's recent email with a very short, simple message. "Bright blessings. Much love, Maya." There was clearly nothing I could say to make her see the truth, and there was nothing more I could do but bless her and let her go. I did my best to clear my energy of any involvement with these issues so I could move on with my life and focus on more important things.

Wisdom from the Angels
The angel session that I had scheduled with Darlene was on the following Friday, and it could not have come at a more perfect time. I was eager to tell her about the minor psychic attack I had been experiencing and ask for her input. The information she shared

during my session was truly fascinating and really rang true for me. And while much of it was related to my own path, she also shared vital information about the Dark Forces and how they operate.

During my talk session with Darlene, I shared everything that had been happening. She took a few moments to tune in intuitively to the situation around Jeffrey. "Yes, he is definitely working with a demon. In fact, he is fully and willingly possessed by this demon. I rarely see full possession such as this."

She looked at me with a serious expression, "He is clearly sourcing energy off of many people, as well as manipulating a whole web of people. Based on what I'm seeing, I recommend that you have absolutely NO contact with him in the future. I recommend even blocking him on Facebook and on your phone so he will have no further way to gain energetic connection with you."

I listened intently, absorbing every word with my pen in hand, taking notes in my journal.

"Maya, you have a tendency to not fully trust yourself and the things you see," she continued, "but you *should* trust yourself. The things you perceive are spot-on correct."

I laughed ruefully and told her how so many people had called me oversensitive over the years, and how I had even gone to a well-known psychic reader who had called me paranoid. Darlene gasped and then laughed out loud with a glimmer of light-hearted understanding in her eye. She explained that most people simply do not see as much as I do, so they just don't understand. It was such a relief to *finally* receive validation from another person about my intense spiritual knowings — specifically, someone I felt was further ahead than me.

"Maya, you need to stand in your truth more firmly. You tend to waffle, sit on the fence, and try to be nice in order to not make waves. I get it. You don't want to stir up conflict. But, when you walk on eggshells with everyone and don't speak what you really mean, you are of service to no one at all. You have been doing this in the recent situation with Jeffrey. You sort of spoke your truth but went out of your way to be diplomatic and try to avoid the situation. What this does is it makes your message less convincing, and even makes it appear that you don't care at all."

"Really?!" I asked, incredulously. I had thought I was preserving everyone's feelings when I was super-diplomatic. It had never occurred to me that it was giving people the impression I didn't care. Wow!

Darlene continued, "Now that you understand this, it is important that you be much more direct from now on, even if it feels scary."

This gave me butterflies in my stomach and made my head spin. I absolutely hated conflict and tried to avoid it at all costs. As a highly sensitive person with a tender heart, conflict felt nearly intolerable to me. I really hated it when people were upset, and especially when they were upset with *me*. I took a deep breath, and mentally promised myself that from now on, I would speak my truth more directly and bravely.

"What about free will?" I asked Darlene. "I go out of my way to honor this in others and encourage them to follow their own inner wisdom. I don't think it would be right for me to go around being the 'ethics police,' outing people in the community. When and with whom should I share information about energy predators, and when should I keep it to myself?"

"If your student was about to jump off a cliff, would you let them?"

"Of course not!"

"Well, then, Maya, if someone tells you they have scheduled a session with a predator, or they're asking about that person, it is your responsibility and duty to be completely direct. Tell them that you suggest they do not go to that person, that they will be putting themselves in danger, and why." Darlene clarified, "You are able to see and sense things that many of your students cannot. Because of this, they do not have the vital information needed. As their mentor, it is your job to share this information with them."

"Okay, I understand now how important it is that I not withhold information from my students. Telling them the vital truth is more important than any worry I might have about making waves." I had struggled a great deal over this issue for a very long time, and I was grateful for her perspective and clarity.

"What about other people? I don't think I should necessarily share the things I know with every single person I meet. For some, it might be considered unsolicited advice. What do you suggest? What would you do in this type of situation?"

"Well," Darlene continued, "When it comes to people in the community, it is not your duty or business to interfere or intervene with every single person out there. However, if the individual is a personal friend or one of your students or clients, then you have a moral duty to warn them if they are about to get involved with a predator."

I nodded, absorbing it all. I recalled a couple of times in my life when friends had withheld certain information from me when I was about to unknowingly get involved in a bad situation. Only after the fact did they come forward, explaining that they had considered telling me, but hesitated to intrude or intervene. I felt betrayed by these friends, as though trust had been broken, since they had knowingly withheld vital information, and in doing so, had allowed me to enter into potentially harmful situations!

It was definitely a tricky issue, the fine line between sharing vital information with those who need it, and giving unsolicited or intrusive advice. When was it right to share with others, and when was it right to keep the information private? I was also someone who tried to avoid gossip at all costs, and even though the information I was sharing was true and exceedingly important, I wanted to avoid any semblance of gossip. I took another deep breath and made an internal vow to always share vital information when it involves my close friends, students, and clients. With other individuals in the community, I would have to use my discernment on a case-by-case basis.

Darlene went on, "The issue of sexual and energetic predators within spiritual communities is much more prevalent than most people realize. I've worked with numerous women who have been victims. There is also major spiritual warfare going on in the spiritual community in our city, very intense battles between light and dark."

My eyes got even bigger, taking it all in.

"Maya, you will be doing a lot of work with shamanism in the future. I've seen the classes you've been offering lately. These classes are not even close to the depth and scope of classes you will be teaching in the future. You will soon be looked upon and sought out as an authority in many areas. People will come to you seeking your opinion, and it is vital that you stand in your truth and communicate clearly and directly."

Wow! It was hard for me to wrap my mind around all of this, but I took it all under consideration. I wondered if what she was saying was true and what types of classes I would be teaching in the future.

Darlene continued sharing her words of wisdom. "In your own spiritual practices, it is best if you work on connecting directly with God. So many people in the New Age community connect with guides and ascended masters. The problem with this is that there are many dark spiritual beings that pretend to be beings of light. You can't go wrong if you connect directly with God for your guidance. Connect with God first, then whatever other guides, angels, etc. you connect with after that will be aligned with God."

I was blown away by this. There were really dark beings that pretended to be spirit guides and ascended masters of light?! I mentally vowed to follow her advice in this regard—to connect directly with the Divine and to be extra cautious with any other spiritual beings I encountered.

I brought myself back to the present moment and looked at Darlene. "I don't understand why all this drama has come into my life when in fact I've worked very hard to cultivate a very peaceful, low-drama life. I don't get it."

Darlene laughed and then got serious. "Well, Maya! You've just had a full-on demon walk into your life! Of course, you've had drama!"

That made me laugh. Of course, that made a lot of sense!

Then, Darlene went on to explain, "Maya, those us who walk so fully in the light are often targeted by the darkness. When I met you briefly more than fifteen years ago, I recognized you immediately as a lightworker, and my angels told me this as well. So often, lightworkers are attacked by demonic energies or tempted or fooled into agreeing to connect with them. And when that does not work, the Dark Forces will send actual people to prey upon us. I experienced psychic attack as a child, and when that was ineffective, the Dark Forces began sending predatory men into my life."

I gasped. That sounded just like my life! Not only had I experienced psychic attack as a child and adult, but I had also been a magnet for sexual predators in my romantic relationships. On top of that, I had been in three different romantic relationships with men who had each been possessed by demonic entities! (Of course, this was never revealed until I was already deeply involved in the relationship.) For years, I had blamed myself, wondering how other women seemed to easily find wonderful men, yet the only men that showed up in my world were completely awful. Through a lot of personal development work, I came to understand that it is common for people who had abusive childhoods to attract abusive romantic partners in adulthood, but it had never occurred to me that the issue could be partly due to my being targeted by the Dark Forces.

Reflecting on my relationships revealed a pattern I had not seen before. In my twenties, I had escaped a relationship with a horrible sociopath. I moved forward with my life, hoping to heal and find a good healthy, relationship. In my early thirties, I was still recovering from serious health issues after living in that haunted farmhouse and being attacked by the evil spirit, as I mentioned in the book's introduction. I had just moved to a new city and was alone and physically ill. From this point of vulnerability, I ended up falling into a relationship with Brent. Things were going well, and we decided to move in together to test the waters and see if we might eventually want to get married. As soon as we moved in together, he was no longer able to hide his true colors. I realized within a couple of weeks that I had made a horrible mistake. He admitted to me that he had been diagnosed with severe bipolar disorder, yet he was unwilling to receive any treatment. He was verbally abusive and controlling, and I fell into a deep depression as I walked on eggshells every single day. One morning, Brent was just coming home from working the night shift. I opened my eyes to see him opening the bedroom door. As he stood in the doorway, I could see him in the dim light of the early morning, yet it was not him. There was an image of a demon superimposed over him, with horrifying facial features and huge ram's horns winding up from his head! I was terrified as he crawled into bed next to me. I escaped that relationship just a few weeks later.

I stayed single for a while after that, trying to hit the reset button so I would attract healthy people into my world. Then, I met Chris. We were never quite the right fit, so we were on again, off again for a few years. The final time we were intimate, I saw his face change before my eyes into the face of a demon with completely black eyes and short stubby horns on top of his head. After that incident, I ended the romantic aspect of our relationship. We shared several friends in common, so we remained on cordial terms. During that time, I saw demons walking through his home on more than one occasion. Even though we were no longer a couple, we had always felt a special closeness like family, which was why I continued to allow him in my world. But eventually, I had to release him completely from my life due to the ongoing demonic activity that kept showing up, and the fact that he was unwilling to face and deal with it.

I chose to stay single for a while, very serious about my commitment to clear the slate and finally be able to bring a truly healthy relationship into my life, one not overshadowed by abuse or dark interference. A few years after that, I was in a relationship with someone I loved very deeply, but who I finally realized was horribly oppressed by dark beings that constantly fed him thoughts of despair and misery. He was a victim of numerous malevolent entity attachments and no matter what I would say to him, the dark beings around him would distort everything that came his way. That relationship broke my heart, and it took me years to recover.

For the next few years, I avoided entering a relationship, intending to stay single until I found someone truly healthy. Then, Jeffrey came along. We had been friends for a few years, and he was now single. Because we had been friends for a while, I felt that we had already established trust, and I felt comfortable moving forward with a romance. And of course, as you already know, that went south very fast! Now, come to find out that Jeffrey, too, has a demonic entity working through him. Ugh!

Darlene knew about my history with Jeffrey, "Maya, the Dark Forces love to attack lightworkers by sending malevolent people into their lives, especially through romantic relationships. Because of this, you absolutely need to be more careful who you get involved with."

I looked at Darlene and gave an exasperated sigh. I felt tears well up in my eyes and I felt a little defensive. "But Darlene, I *have* tried to be careful! Every time I've chosen to get involved with someone, it has always been with a level head and measured consideration. Only later I would find out that the person had serious psychological or spiritual issues. And I don't even date casually! I'm more careful than anyone I know about dating and intimacy, and at this point, I haven't even dated at all for over two years!"

Her eyes got big as she nodded with understanding, realizing how much the Dark Forces had attacked me again and again through romantic relationships. I felt the tears burning my eyes. For years, I had beat myself up, feeling like somehow it was all my fault, that there was something wrong with me or my vibration that I could be attracting such people. But now I was realizing I was not completely to blame. I am a servant of the light, and because of that, I had been targeted for attack again and again by the Dark Forces.

Darlene looked at me with compassion and wisdom.

"Maya, you are stepping up into a new level of personal power and confidence, standing even more strongly in the light than ever before. As you do this, you will be able to stand more fully in your truth, and the darkness will not be able to touch you. There is one thing the darkness often fails to understand — that when it attacks or pushes us, it only serves to make us stronger!"

LESSON 5 – THE SYMPTOMS OF PSYCHIC ATTACK

A psychic attack can include any type of interference in your energy. As we discussed in chapter one, a psychic attack can originate from any number of sources, from a jealous or angry person unintentionally sending negative vibes your way, to a person intentionally casting a harmful magickal spell against you, to minor disruptions from an annoying spirit, to a full-out attack by a malevolent spiritual entity. No matter the source, the symptoms of psychic attack are similar, yet the symptoms can vary from case to case and person to person.

Below you will find a comprehensive list of common symptoms of psychic attack. Many of the personal symptoms can be caused by normal circumstances, like everyday stress, worry, normal physical illness, mental health issues, etc., and many of the environmental symptoms can be caused by easily explainable phenomenon, like house settling, actual electrical issues in the home, cool breezes caused by a draft, etc. Once normal causes are ruled out, you can begin to consider that energetic or paranormal origins may be to blame. (If you are having any type of physical or mental health issue, be sure to consult your medical professional.)

As you go through the checklist below, keep in mind that even having just one symptom can indicate you're under psychic attack. In other words, a person can be experiencing a severe psychic attack and only have one symptom on the list. On the contrary, a person can have numerous symptoms on the list, but because the symptoms are mild in nature, the attack is a mild one. Going through the checklist will help you identify whether you're experiencing a psychic attack, but you will also need to weigh the severity of each symptom as you determine whether it is a mild, moderate, or severe situation.

<u>Evaluation Instructions:</u>

Next to each issue, write a number 0-5 to indicate the extent you are experiencing that issue, with 0 indicating not at all, and 5 indicating a severe issue.

Mental/Emotional Effects:

_____ Nightmares, especially dreams of being attacked or chased

_____ Fear of going to sleep

_____ Feeling of extreme fear or dread

_____ Mental disorientation

_____ Forgetfulness, trouble focusing, or 'brain fog'

_____ Moodiness or on edge

_____ Feeling angry for no apparent reason

_____ Apathy, or lack of interest in life

_____ Anxiety or worry

_____ Sudden onset of depression

_____ Obsessive thoughts

_____ Having unusually dark thoughts that don't seem to be your own

_____ Nervous exhaustion or mental breakdown

_____ Feeling like you are going crazy and/or

questioning your sanity

_____ Worsening of addictive behaviors

_____ Loss of self-confidence

_____ Self-destructive thoughts, or suicidal thoughts

_____ Substance abuse, or relapse of substance abuse or other addictive behavior

_____ Thoughts, feelings, or urges that are uncharacteristic for you

_____ Suddenly acting out of character

Physical Well-Being Effects:

_____ Trouble sleeping

_____ Coughing, choking, or feeling like you cannot breathe

_____ Dizziness or vertigo

_____ Headache

_____ Stomachache, nausea, or cramping

_____ Accident-prone

_____ Car accident or other significant accident

_____ Unexplainable exhaustion

_____ Sudden onset of illness (can be an explainable illness like cancer, or a condition that evades diagnosis)

_____ Unexplainable pain in part of or all of the body

_____ Sexual impotence

_____ Change in appetite, no appetite, or overeating

_____ Wake up in the morning feeling drained

_____ Unexplainable bruising

_____ Feel better after a shower or bath

Physical Experiences:

_____ Sleep paralysis

_____ Feeling of weight on your chest

_____ Foul stench from unknown origin, may smell like sulfur, something rotting, or other horrible smell

_____ Feeling of being physically touched, attacked, molested, or sexually assaulted by an unseen source

_____ Feeling icy-cold for no apparent reason

_____ Feeling like something is touching you

_____ Hair stands up on the back of your neck, or you get chills down your spine

_____ Feeling like you are being watched

_____ Missing time (a gap in memory for a certain time period, can be minutes, hours, or days)

_____ Reality seems to bend. Odd things occur that make no sense.

Life Issues:

_____ Unusually bad luck in finances, relationships, career, or other areas of life

_____ Upsurge of drama in your life

_____ Challenging life situations such as divorce, loss of job, death in the family, etc.

_____ Unusual amount of interpersonal conflict in your life

_____ Bank account has been hacked, identity theft, loss of a large amount of money, or going through bankruptcy

_____ A family member or pet becomes unexplainably ill or dies

Issues in Physical Environment:

_____ Items going missing from home

_____ Electronic devices breaking or acting strange

_____ Lights flashing

_____ Odd temperature fluctuations in the home, especially cold spots

_____ Hearing unusual sounds in the home, including

knocking, creaking, disembodied voices, etc.

_____ Seeing apparitions — ghosts, demons, or other spiritual beings

_____ Physical objects moving for no explainable reason

_____ Feel uncomfortable in one part of your home

_____ Seeing shadows, or feeling like you see something out of the corner of your eye, but when you turn to look, nothing is there

Assessing Your Results

Add up your results from your evaluation so you have one final number. It is quite challenging to create a 'grading scale' for this evaluation because some items on the list are quite obviously indications of psychic attack (like seeing a malevolent spirit and literally being attacked by it), compared to more subtle experiences. If you are having an obvious, severe situation, you already know that you are under attack. For those of you experiencing more subtle, difficult to identify issues, this evaluation scale can be helpful.

0-5—It is unlikely that you are under any sort of psychic attack, but it will not hurt to do some clearing and protection techniques just in case.

5-10—It is possible that you may be under psychic attack. Go ahead and do some clearing and protection techniques so you are on the safe side.

10-15—It is likely you are under moderate psychic attack. As soon as possible, perform clearing and protection techniques.

15 and up—It is likely you are under severe psychic attack. Immediately employ the most powerful clearing and protection techniques you can and seek the help of a psychic protection professional. •

As you ponder your results from this survey, keep in mind that some psychic attacks can come on very strongly and suddenly, while others can be quite subtle and come on gradually. Extreme psychic attacks tend to be more obvious, while subtle psychic attacks can sometimes be difficult to identify. One of my students calls the subtle type of psychic attack a "slow burn psychic attack" because it can go on for months or even years without being fully recognized. I have noticed that as human beings, we tend to avoid truths that feel uncomfortable, so even when we have evidence of a psychic attack right in front of us, we do not want to admit what is really happening. It is time to do an honest evaluation and look at what is really occurring in your life. Are there any indications of psychic attack in your life? (Or have there been any indications in the past?) If so, do not despair. As you read on, you will obtain more knowledge about how psychic attacks work and how you can clear and protect yourself.

CHAPTER 6 - ANGEL HEALING

Healing from the Angels?

About a week after my private session with Darlene, I attended one of her Angel Healing Group Sessions. Darlene sat in front of the group and shared her story about how she had started working with angels more than forty years ago. Her very personal story captivated everyone in attendance. She described how she had fallen into a very debilitating emotional despair and crippling agoraphobia that kept her homebound and in bed for days at a time, unable to function in daily life. One day, in utter desperation, she sat on the edge of her bed and cried out to God, "Please, I just want to stop feeling so horrible. Please help me." As soon as those words were spoken, Archangel Michael appeared before her, and then a choir of archangels filled the room. She blinked, then blinked again, thinking she was imagining things. But the angels still remained. Since that encounter so many years ago, she had been receiving and sharing messages and healing energy from these angels and had centered her life around serving this cause.

Darlene then explained that during the group session she would call in the archangels and their special energy would enter each person for healing purposes. She then held up a thick hardback book and a beautiful silver pin. The pin was an angel with wings outstretched and holding an opalescent stone in her open hands. The stone reminded me of a miniature crystal ball. The book, which was about Darlene and her angel encounters, had a large image of the angel pin on the cover.

"Some people choose to buy the pin or the book so the items can be infused with the healing energy of the angels during your session. I commissioned a dear artist friend of mine in Sedona to design this pin for me, and she has been kind enough to duplicate it so that my students and clients can have their own as well. This pin is protective and healing, so I encourage you to wear it as often as you can in order to obtain the benefits. Let's take a short break now so anyone who wants to make a purchase may do so."

A couple of us filed out into the hallway to get a closer look at the books and angel pins. I picked out a book, chose my pin with special care, made my purchase, and pinned the angel to my shirt before rejoining the group. Each person found a cozy place on the floor, creating personal nesting areas with yoga mats, pillows, and blankets as we settled in to receive the angel healing.

During the session, I felt a lot of energy and pressure in and around my throat, and then I felt a warmth flowing through different parts of my body, including my sore shoulder. A few times during the session, I opened my eyes to peek. Darlene was standing in the front of the room with her arms raised. I did not see any angels, but I did see a soft red light gently streaming throughout the room.

Immediately after the session, I tuned into myself and

noticed that I felt pretty balanced and calm. Some of the attendees stayed after for a while to chat. I started an interesting conversation with a young woman who was an energy healer, but after a while I felt a bit uncomfortable. She seemed to be throwing condescending verbal jabs at me left and right, all while smiling and speaking in a soft ultra-spiritual tone of voice. A number of times, she mentioned in a boasting voice that she was mentoring with Darlene. I was a little confused by this since I did not see Darlene as someone who would attract students that were so ego-driven. As I stood there, I sent the young woman some love, knowing that her condescending attitude was most likely coming from insecurity. Eventually, I politely extracted myself from the conversation and drove home.

I went straight to bed and pinned my angel on my bedside lampshade for protection. But sleep was unusually restless. I felt sick, like I was coming down with the flu. My body felt shaky and weak, and my cat was acting oddly out of sorts, literally trying to sit on my pillow, pushing her body against the top of my head. I did not want her on my head. I pushed her off, so she then repositioned herself on my stomach. Every time I woke from my fitful sleep, I would open my eyes to see her sitting up on my stomach, with a worried cat expression looking directly at my face. By morning, she started climbing all over me, using her paws to move my arms into different positions. She is normally a very interactive and protective cat who will try to take care of me when I am upset or not feeling well, but this behavior was just beyond weird.

The next morning, I woke a little tired, but everything seemed fine throughout the day. That night, I slept fine, but the following morning, things took a bizarre turn. I woke up to the sound of my alarm. Sleepily opening my eyes, I clairvoyantly saw a large creature standing beside my bed. Due to his appearance, I immediately assumed he was some sort of earth elemental. His skin was grayish, he had a friendly human-looking face, and he had short, pointy animal ears on top of his head. He was so tall that he was bent perpendicular at his hips with his head turned sideways, looking right at me with an expression of curiosity. Even though he did not look threatening, I did not want him there. I prayed to Archangel Michael to please remove him. Trusting that would be the end of it, I hit the snooze button and closed my eyes.

Ten minutes later, my alarm went off again. I opened my eyes, and was so startled, I yelled, "Ahh!" The tall, gray elemental was still there in the very same place, bent over looking right at me. Once again, I hit the snooze button, closed my eyes, and spoke out loud in a groggy voice, "I'm not comfortable with you being here. Please leave right now!" Then, I fell back to sleep. (Yes, I am that good at falling asleep.) When my alarm went off once again, I cautiously opened my eyes. The elemental creature was still there, and now there were other beings in the room, too. There was a blonde, human-sized woman in a unique flowing white dress that had white light shining from it, as though there were LED lights within the dress shining in different lines down the length of the floor-length dress. Around this woman swirled a fantasia of small fairies and other elementals flying around the room. I heard the word "leader," which led me to believe that the blonde woman was the leader of these other beings.

I continued to recline in bed, considering what it was that I was seeing. Maybe the recent angel healing session had opened up my clairvoyance even more. I was not sure what to think of this experience. I was used to seeing glimpses of angels, of spirits, of colors and energies in the energy fields of my clients, and even fairies from time to time. But I had never seen anything like this, and certainly not for this length of time. I was no stranger to spiritual visions, but this was unusual, even for me. Eventually, the experience subsided and I got up to start my day. I assumed that it was just a fluke strange experience and I put it to the back of my mind.

Later that day, I looked at my phone and saw that I had received an email from Groupon. I ignored it. About an hour later, a duplicate email came through, and I ignored that one, too. About an hour after that, a third email came through from Groupon, and this time, I opened it. My mouth dropped. It was an advertisement for fairy LED lights. I thought that was kind of an odd coincidence and it gave me the creeps. I had written about the recent fairy experience in my journal while I was sitting outside under a tree, but other than that, I had not told a soul about my experience. One odd thing that had stood out, though, was that as I had been sitting outside writing about the recent fairy experience in my journal, there were two unusual black crows in my backyard. One in particular would fly down and sit on the power line and loudly squawk on and on at my black cat. The other crow perched in the tree and looked sideways at me while I wrote. Both crows gave me a very strange feeling like I was being watched, and I immediately thought of Anne when I looked into their eyes. The thought had crossed my mind that Anne had used black magick to keep an eye on me through these strangely acting crows. Something in my inner guidance was telling me that I was under surveillance. That thought was just way too strange, though, so I put it out of my mind, assuming I must be overreacting.

As I looked at the advertisement for fairy LED lights, I suddenly recalled some other strange occurrences. Back when Anne had her open house at the center, I had commented on how much I loved her bell fountain. It was a large brass bowl with stationary brass bells and moving brass bells that float on the flowing water, causing the moving bells to softly strike against the stationary ones at random intervals. As soon as I saw it, I fell in love with it and proclaimed that I wanted to get one for myself. We talked about how they can be ordered off of Amazon.com and how I intended to order one very soon. When I got home that evening and checked my email, there was an advertisement in the sidebar of my email browser. The ad was for the exact fountain on Amazon that Anne and I had been discussing. I am fully aware that our purchases and internet searches are tracked and that this information is used to inform the advertisements that show up in our internet browser, email, and social media. However, I was 100% sure that I had never searched for that item online before, and I was fully certain that that ad had never once shown up on my computer until that day. One friend pointed out that Facebook and other apps on our phone utilize our phone microphone and camera to collect information about us. I was not sure if this was true or not, but I would not be surprised if it was. At the time, I thought the situation was kind of odd, but I decided to brush it off as a weird coincidence.

A week after the bell fountain situation, I was teaching a workshop at my home. While I was teaching, I happened to mention the movie, "The Secret," and how it had confused and misled a lot of people through oversimplified teachings about The Law of Attraction. Later that night, "The Secret," was prominently featured in my sidebar ads. No, I had never done an internet search for it, and no, it has never shown up in my ads before, ever. I did have my phone with me while I was teaching, so I thought it might be possible that the information had been picked up by my phone's microphone. I was not sure if it was relevant or not, but I pondered how Anne had been present during the bell fountain conversation, and she had also been present in the class when I had talked about "The Secret."

After the odd coincidence regarding "The Secret," I decided to try a little experiment to see if my ads were being directed by words that my microphone was picking up. I held my phone in my hand and repeated the word, "screwdriver," multiple times, with varying sentences, like, "I need a screwdriver for a project I'm doing," "I'm looking for a screwdriver," etc. No screwdrivers showed up on my online ads. After that, I decided to let it go...until I saw the ad about the LED fairy lights. It was just too weird! I was suddenly filled with a sensation of paranoia and an overwhelming feeling that I was being watched. I called my friend Raina to tell her what was going on.

"Am I just being paranoid??" I asked, my voice a bit panicky.

"Maya, just because you're paranoid doesn't mean you're wrong."

LESSON 6–TWO SIGNS THAT NEGATIVE ENERGIES ARE PLUGGING INTO YOU

You as the reader may have already figured out that there was something suspicious about Darlene and the angel pin. The truth is, when I was going through this whole situation, I did not suspect anything, at least not at first. That is how this kind of thing works. You get pulled into the spell. And besides, most of us tend to assume the best about other people. As you continue reading the story, you will find out the shocking ways I began to suspect something was up with Darlene. But for now, let's focus on two very important signs that negative energies are plugging into you.

To be clear, this was not information I knew about at this point in the story. One of my mentors explained it to me after this psychic attack was complete, and when she did, I immediately knew within every cell of my being that it was absolute truth. The first sign of entity attachment is that you feel unusually unwell. The second sign is that you feel absolutely wonderful.

Sign #1: Feeling Unwell

Obviously, everyone feels unwell for normal, natural reasons now and then, and not all occurrences are indications of psychic attack. Sometimes, it is quite difficult to uncover the reason you are feeling unwell, and often the psychic attack is only obvious after the fact. If you are feeling unwell, it is always best to consider medical causes first and seek medical advice. When symptoms come on literally out of the blue and have no known logical reason, it is a surefire sign that a negative energy has just plugged into you.

Simply put, there are three types of negative energies that may be making an energetic connection. Either someone has sent negative energy via a spell or curse, a person is hooking energy cords into you, or an actual malevolent entity is plugging into your energy field. When this low-vibration, negative energy plugs into your energy field, it lowers your vibration quite a bit in a relatively short period of time. Sometimes the negative energy shift occurs immediately, and sometimes there is a bit of a delayed effect. But, when it happens, it can cause dizziness, vertigo, nausea, stomachache, headache, shakiness, chills, hot flash, weakness, lightheadedness, mental fog, flu-like symptoms, or sudden depression or anxiety.

Anytime your vibration shifts dramatically over a short span of time, you will feel it. After a negative energy connects, the person will either feel inexplicably ill for a long period of time, or they will feel ill for a brief period before their system partially adapts to the malevolent energy attachment. If your system adapts, that does not mean you are in the clear. It simply means you are steadily leaking life force energy and your energy body is frantically trying to find ways to adapt. This is one way that chronic illnesses can gradually take hold of a person.

I have a few very potent examples of negative energy

attachment causing feelings of illness. Note that I felt very ill the night I obtained the angel pin and brought it home. I felt shaky, feverish, and very weak, yet the next day, the severe symptoms had subsided. This was because a dark entity had plugged into my energy during the so-called angel healing. In this case, there was a slightly delayed effect. I felt fine during the angel session yet horrible a few hours later. Once I was relaxed and asleep (vulnerable), the dark being began to connect more deeply and suck life force energy from me. By the following day, my body had somewhat adapted to having a steady stream of life force energy leaking from me. The more severe physical symptoms were replaced with a steady exhaustion. I did not understand what had happened, so I did not know to clear the attachment (until later).

In chapter 3, I talked about my very brief romantic interlude with Jeffrey. We were only intimate a couple of times, and in hindsight, our first encounter was an obvious indication of energy attachment. About five minutes after, we were lying in my bed relaxing and talking. I was on my back staring up at the ceiling when all of a sudden, the ceiling started spinning. It stopped after a moment, and I thought, "Whoa! What was that?" I turned onto my side, then all of a sudden, I was overcome by extreme, overwhelming vertigo. I squeezed my eyes shut but the spinning did not stop. If you have ever had severe vertigo, you know how horrible it can be. The vertigo continued non-stop. After about ten minutes, Jeffrey said he really needed to go. I stayed there in bed for another twelve hours, completely unable to move or turn my head.

Eventually, the vertigo subsided enough that I could stand up without falling down and walk myself to the bathroom. I was a little annoyed that Jeffrey had not stayed longer to assist me, but since we had been friends for such a long time, I let it go.

The next day, I consulted with an energy healer who had been working with me long-distance for many years. When I told her what had happened, she said the vertigo was a positive symptom of my body going through spiritual ascension and my vibration going up. In other words, she was saying that the vertigo was an indication of something good. Because I trusted her and felt she was more experienced than me, I took her word for it and did not suspect a thing. In hindsight, I do believe she meant well and that she actually believed what she had told me. But now, knowing what I know about Jeffrey and psychic protection in general, I am positive without a doubt that the vertigo was directly caused by numerous energy cords that had attached via sexual intercourse, causing my vibration to plummet down, down, down as my life force was tapped into. In fact, for months afterward, I felt exhausted and ill and had no idea why. Now I know.

Sign #2: Feeling Wonderful

Most people assume that everything is A-okay when they are feeling wonderful. How could feeling good be a *bad* thing, right? People are often shocked when I explain this concept to them. Feelings of bliss and ecstasy are actually an indication that negative energies are hooking into you. Here's how it works:

One of the most insidious ways dark energies hook into people is by utilizing something called 'spiritual anesthetic.' Coined by my mentor, Holly, spiritual anesthetic is when a malevolent entity attaches to a person, it will emit something that not only numbs the area but also produces feelings of bliss and ecstasy. The unsuspecting victim is feeling so good, they have no idea what is really happening to them. It is similar to when a leech attaches onto a person to suck blood. The leech produces an anesthetic so that the person won't notice anything has latched onto them.

This is a common occurrence at spiritual events — especially those that feature concepts of universal oneness, non-resistance, personal bliss, or channeling of unknown spiritual beings. In these circumstances, the participants and facilitators are not using good discernment regarding the energies and entities they are calling in, and as such, they end up drawing in either dark beings or false light beings. Dark beings are entities that have malevolent intent. False light beings are actually dark beings that are disguised as light beings in order to trick unsuspecting victims. Unfortunately, being self-protective is often discouraged in many spiritual circles, so attendees end up blindly following without question. Because the concept of oneness is greatly emphasized (and personal boundaries and discernment are often shamed), participants are encouraged to open their energy up completely during the group spiritual activity, leaving the participants completely vulnerable to entity attachments of all kinds.

Because of what I now know from my own firsthand experience and what I've learned from my mentors, I am now exceedingly careful when I attend spiritual events. Now let me be clear. There is nothing wrong with spiritual events, chanting, sound healing concerts, group meditation, and the like. These can all be wonderful things, if the facilitators use proper procedures and have an awareness of psychic protection issues. But, more often than not, these spiritual activities end up being a hotbed for entity attachments using spiritual anesthetic.

I advise extreme caution, especially when attending sound healing concerts. Sound healing involves the use of either musical instruments or electronic devices to produce certain sounds and frequencies, many of which have tremendous impact on the human energy field. I have personal friends who are sound healers, and I love the experience of sound healing! Many tones and frequencies can be tremendously healing, and some have even been studied for their ability to heal cancer and repair DNA. Yet, used in a group forum, these tones and sounds tend to open everyone's energy field, providing easy access for malevolent attachment.

I have personally attended many wonderful sound healing events, and yet, I have also attended a few that were outright dangerous. One such negative sound healing concert took place about five years ago at a local healing center. It was clear from meeting the sound artists that they were well-meaning but were inexperienced and had little actual knowledge about the impact of the tones they were using. The healing center was packed full with eager participants. When the concert started, we all closed our eyes to immerse ourselves in the sound bath. I immediately fell ill, while everyone around me was transported by feelings of utter bliss. My head started spinning and I felt like I wanted to jump out of my skin. I opened my eyes and saw an energy portal open in the center of the room and all sorts of beings began coming through.

After a few more minutes, I quietly got up and left. Everyone had their eyes closed, so my exit was unnoticed until the concert ended. The owner of the healing center had noticed my absence and messaged me with genuine concern, wanting to know if I was okay, and expressing how much everyone was raving about their blissed-out experience at the concert.

Let me be perfectly clear. It is completely fine to feel uplifted, inspired, grounded, and centered at a spiritual event. But if you suddenly feel ill, or if you are, out of the blue, overcome by feelings of bliss and ecstasy, get the heck out of there! Don't worry that people will think you're being rude for leaving. Don't worry if people think you're overreacting or way off base. If you are suddenly overcome with feelings or sensations you were not having before, chances are, entities are in the process of hooking into you. *You* are responsible for the welfare of your own energy. Do not expect the event facilitators to take proper care of your spiritual welfare, because, unfortunately, many people simply do not have a clue what they are doing to their event participants.

Losing a Friend

Here is another example of spiritual anesthesia. My former friend, Roxi, used to frequently attend group classes and one-on-one sessions with a local healer named Katie. Since Roxi was a close friend of mine, I privately warned her that Katie was deeply involved with False Light beings. I told Roxi that in my professional opinion, I felt she was putting herself in serious danger by associating with this healer, and that if she had any further contact, she should do so with extreme caution. As a friend, I will share my opinion when I am guided to, but I recognize that each person has the free will to choose what is best for them.

"Wow, thank you for telling me about this, Maya!" Roxi said, then furrowed her brow thoughtfully. "But, I truly feel amazing and blissful when I go to her classes and sessions! How can that be a bad thing?"

I explained spiritual anesthetic to her, and her eyes got really big.

"Really?" Her brow furrowed more deeply as she considered everything I said. "Well, I'm going to still keep going to her. I think she's fine."

That was her decision, so I let it go and hoped for the best.

The next time I saw Roxi she was attending one of my

group classes. Roxi's eyes were glazed over and she was acting truly weird! I asked her if she was okay, and she proclaimed in a robot voice, "I feel wonderful! I had such a powerful healing session a couple days ago from Katie." She then walked around to all the students in the class and insisted on hugging every single person. I watched Roxi as she hooked into each person's energy, thus giving secondary access to the entities working through Katie. I was pissed she was doing that because I do *not* allow that in my classes! I calmly went around the group and removed all energy that had been implanted, then went on with teaching.

Fast forward a couple more weeks. Roxi's behavior quickly became more and more erratic. Apparently, the spiritual bliss was wearing off. She began lashing out at me quite regularly, twisting everything I said. We sat down and had a talk one day after she had done some particularly cruel and out of character things toward me. I asked her what was going on, and she admitted that she was constantly hearing a voice in her head telling her all sorts of terrible things — terrible things about herself and terrible things about me. She said she could no longer control herself, and she did not know why she was lashing out at me so badly.

I gently explained the concept of spiritual anesthetic to her again, and I told her point blank that I believed her emotional upheaval (bliss followed by toxic mental activity) was a direct result of entity attachments from her sessions with Katie. I helped her use a pendulum to check if she had any attachments, and if so, how many. She tested as having more than one hundred energy cords connected to her! I helped her do a powerful technique to remove the attachments. She immediately felt nauseous as the entities disconnected, allowing her vibration to quickly shift back up to a healthier state.

Unfortunately, soon after, Roxi decided to resume going to Katie's classes and sessions, and as soon as she did, Roxi's behavior toward me became even more hostile. Sadly, I eventually had to distance myself from Roxi due to ongoing toxic behavior, personal attacks toward me, and unwillingness to steer clear of the entity attachments that were causing the issues. She had become addicted to the bliss the entities were providing her, despite the fact that they were also mentally torturing her. While I wholeheartedly support a person's right to choose what's right for them, if their behavior becomes outright abusive, I may unfortunately have to let that person go. After making sincere attempts at loving, healthy communication, and giving Roxi several opportunities to discontinue the abusive behavior, I finally chose to release Roxi as a friend. I was sad for her, but understood that she had become too brainwashed to understand what was really happening.

Recap
Anytime you are suddenly filled with out-of-the-ordinary sensations or feelings, this is a strong indication that one or more entities are in the process of attaching into you or have already attached into you. These sensations can include feeling physically or mentally unwell or feeling bliss and ecstasy. When participating in any type of spiritual pursuit whether it

is solo or with a group, you should be feeling clear, grounded, centered, and gently inspired. Pay attention to how you are feeling at all times. Your physical body and your emotions are good barometers for your spiritual safety and well-being. If anything feels out of sorts, discontinue that activity, and immediately begin doing an activity to help you balance, ground, and clear your energy.

People Who Get Angry About This Teaching

I have noticed there are two categories of people who get angry and defensive when I talk about spiritual anesthetic. The first category are those who, like Roxi, are hooked into the dark matrix. They do not want to believe that the concept of spiritual anesthetic is real because they have become addicted to the false bliss being fed to them via their entity attachments. The second category are spiritual teachers, energy healers, channelers, healing center owners, and the like who are greatly benefiting from working with false light entities, as it is bringing them students, followers, and financial gain. Those in this category will often respond with defensiveness, anger, and even attempts to sabotage and ruin the reputation of the person speaking out about spiritual anesthetic. They are afraid that the real truth about their work and livelihood are at risk of being exposed, and they will do whatever it takes to keep the truth hidden. Behind all of this are false light entities that are running the show by influencing and controlling everyone in their web. The ultimate goal of the false light entities is to keep their dark agenda hidden.

CHAPTER 7- DEMON ATTACK

Violated...Again

That Saturday night, I had a very disturbing dream. In the dream, my soul was flying through the spirit realm as three powerful entities were trying to attack me. With their mouths, they were trying to suck all the energy from my crown chakra, my connection with the Divine. It was serious spiritual warfare as I fought back and tried to escape from these evil beings.

I woke up abruptly as I felt my body having an orgasm. As I opened my eyes, I was shocked to see an actual demon standing right next to my bed! The demon had Jeffrey's face and physical build, yet he had small horns protruding from its head. His skin was gray, hairless, and sort of rubbery-looking. The demon was completely naked and had a full erection. I immediately realized that Jeffrey's demon had been messing with me sexually to try to feed off my energy!

I was a bit disoriented. I got up to go to the bathroom, came back to bed and said some prayers for protection, then the next thing I knew, it was morning. As soon as I woke up, I was completely freaked out! How could I have been attacked like that? I had been doing all the standard practices for spiritual protection that I had always done before, so how was this attack able to get through? Why did this happen? And how did this happen? Obviously, I was not protected! Would this happen again? I felt completely vulnerable and scared.

I was supposed to teach a four-hour workshop that afternoon, so I got to work clearing and protecting myself, my home, and my yard. I tried to think of any objects Jeffrey had given me when we had been friends, objects that might be giving him direct access to me or my home. Oh my God. He gave me plants which are now all over the yard! I knew my landlady would not want me digging the plants out, so I went outside and put a hematite gemstone next to each plant, drew Reiki symbols over each one, and prayed that all negative energy be removed. I smudged the whole house with sage and found some powerful sound healing angel music that I played in a loop for several hours.

I went outside and meditated and prayed. When I came back inside, the house felt really good to me, very peaceful and clear. I tuned in to make sure all my students would be safe and free from any sort of negative interference. Immediately, I received the answer that the attack was focused solely on me and that my students would not be interfered with in any way.

The workshop went really well. Energetically, I could feel that the attack was being held at bay the entire time the students were present. Afterward, one of my friends who had attended my class invited me to go out to dinner at Panera Bread. As we sat there chatting and eating, I felt Jeffrey's demon appear on my right side and plug into my root chakra. (In this instance, I did not see him, but I felt his presence.) I saw my friend's mouth moving, but I could barely understand what she was saying. I was suddenly so sleepy and exhausted that I could have fallen asleep right there at the restaurant!

When I got home, I was too nervous to go to sleep, so I sat there, exhausted, watching Netflix until 1:00 a.m. When I finally got into bed, I set my alarm for 7 a.m. so I could take my morning medication. I think I fell asleep as soon as my head hit the pillow.

I slept very deeply, and when I woke, the sun was shining brightly through the window. My bedroom was hot, and it felt late, like it was afternoon. I don't normally sleep into the afternoon. I looked at my analog clock beside my bed and it said 1:30. I was totally confused how I had slept so unusually late, and why my 7 a.m. alarm had not gone off. Had I slept through it? That would be unusual for me because I am not that deep of a sleeper. So, I got up and went to into my living room to check the time on my phone. My phone said 8:30 a.m. Weird. The sun seemed higher than 8:30 a.m. And besides, that would mean I had gotten less than my usual required amount of sleep, yet I felt like I had slept ten to twelve hours.

According to my phone, I had not gotten enough sleep, so I decided to go back to bed for a few hours to avoid being exhausted later in the day. I reset my alarm clock to the correct time (without changing or adjusting the battery at all), and then set my alarm for 10:30 a.m. When I woke to my alarm a couple hours later, the weather was completely different. The sky was dark. Rain was coming down in sheets and it was storming. My alarm clock seemed to be working perfectly and continued to work perfectly thereafter. I had gone to bed a little after 1:00 a.m. Could the clock have stopped at 1:30 a.m. right after I had fallen asleep? Or was it actually 1:30 p.m. the next day when I woke up? Either way, I felt like I had been in some type of time warp.

I had heard about the concept of missing time, when people are abducted by aliens or other unseen forces, only to be returned to the wrong time. Honestly, I was not really considering anything about alien abduction. However, I was indeed concerned about supernatural events causing my time to get so jumbled up. Had I been taken, and then returned to the incorrect time, then lined back up with the correct time when I had slept again? Or, was I in an alternate timeline? I decided right then and there that I would not be sharing this with very many people, except for a few close friends because it sounded impossible and crazy! But, then again, I realized that the entire situation sounded crazy!

When I told my friend Raina what had happened with the sense of displaced time, she asked, "Was your bedside clock inside or outside your circle of salt?" She knew I had placed a circle of salt around my bed for added protection that night.

"It was outside the circle," I responded. I had put the salt around my bed and even in between my sheets, but not around my bedside table.

"Well, Maya, things could have occurred outside your circle of salt, having an effect on the time, yet time would have been different for you inside your circle of salt."

I texted Darlene and told her what was happening, and she said she would do a distant clearing for me that night. The next day, we talked on the phone and she told me what she had seen during the session. She said she'd been surprised that I had still been having issues with psychic attack from Jeffrey because she had already cleared me the week prior. But, during the distant session, she had searched my energy even more persistently and had found three thin black threads (energy cords) that were so well hidden, they were barely detectable. In her opinion, only a highly trained dark master would know how to attach energy cords so skillfully. She said that she did not know any healers besides herself who would know how to find and clear such energies.

That night when I went to bed, I did not feel Jeffrey's energy anymore, but I felt something new. It was a demon hovering above my crown chakra trying to block my connection to the Divine and also keeping an eye on me. I had the strong knowing that this was an entity further up the demonic hierarchy than Jeffrey's demon, as though it was Jeffrey's supervisor, that Jeffrey had not succeeded in his mission so they were sending in the big guns.

The Angel Connection

I scheduled another session with Darlene for Friday morning. When I arrived, I was exhausted from all the recent spiritual warfare, but she assured me that now that the Dark Forces know that I am under her protection, they wouldn't mess with me anymore. Darlene explained that she is a powerful angel in human form, and as such, she is able to have a stronger impact in the physical realm compared to angels in spirit.

I decided to share something very private with her. "Darlene, I have felt connected with angels my whole life, and even as a child, I felt like there was some very important mission I am supposed to accomplish related to God, but I never knew exactly what it was. Even during times in my life when I wasn't sure how to connect with God or even who God was, I still felt (and feel) that strong conviction and total commitment to God, and a mission that I don't even understand."

Darlene paused for a moment then replied, "I feel you are far enough along in your development that I can share this with you. When I first met you many years ago at a psychic fair, I instantly recognized your bright light and that you were very special. Back then, the angels told me that you are an angel incarnate. I now believe that you are one of the twelve angels who will come together to accomplish an important mission here on earth."

What she said was intriguing, but I wasn't sure if it was true for me. I am an open-minded skeptic, so I decided to remain open to possibilities even though it didn't quite ring true for me.

During my session, Darlene counseled me and also shared important information about the hierarchy of demons. "There are four main types of demons," Darlene explained. "The first type of demon are the bottom dwellers. These are the least intelligent and least powerful and are like low vibration creatures. The second type of demon, the gray demons, also called lesser demons, are more intelligent and more powerful than the bottom dwellers. Gray demons have one foot in the human realm and one foot in the spiritual realm. They are the worker bees. These gray demons are the ones who will often possess humans. They frequently possess healers, massage therapists, and spiritual teachers. They look to possess the human beings who have a bright, shiny energy they can feed off of. The gray demons are adept at masquerading as beings of light."

Darlene then went on to describe the two upper levels of demons. "The next level up the hierarchy are called general demons. They are literally the generals who orchestrate what the lesser demons do. Because they are completely devoid of light, when this level of demon possesses a human, it is much like the horror movies where the victim goes into convulsions, speaks in ancient foreign tongues, performs inhuman physical contortions, and more. Finally, the uppermost demons on the hierarchy are even darker than the other levels. They are primordial, as old as creation itself. They exist only in the Hell realm and are rarely on Earth."

Darlene went on to describe another demonic creature called the hellhound. "A hellhound is a cross between a pit bull and a lion that will jump on a person's back and claw in to feed off the person's heart energy. These hellhounds run in pairs and are called Andragonis. I've personally encountered hellhounds, and believe me, you do not want to mess with these creatures."

After we went through the different types of demonic beings, we switched gears again. "Darlene, I have a question. Yesterday, I was driving to go see my sister. I passed a McDonald's on the way, and I literally saw several demons flying in a circle over that place. What does this mean?"

"Well, essentially, you are seeing a lot more demonic energy in your field of vision. Those things were there before, but you just were not seeing them. Now that you're more aware, it seems like you're seeing this stuff everywhere. You've flipped to one side of the spectrum. Eventually, it will settle down and you will only see such things when you are supposed to, when it is necessary for safety or to assist someone."

My head was swimming with all this new information. I was trying to wrap my mind around all of these things that I was learning, and all that was happening. It felt like my life had become a Dan Brown novel of spiritual intrigue. After the session, I went home and picked an oracle card for guidance. The message on the card was, "Your choices are yours to make. Don't let others choose for you. Don't give your power away."

LESSON 7 – PSYCHIC PROTECTION AT NIGHT

Nighttime is a time when we are generally more vulnerable to psychic attack. While psychic attack does indeed occur during the daylight hours, there are unique aspects of nighttime that make it a prime time for negative spiritual activity.

First of all, when you are sleeping, you are not conscious of what is going on around you. In this vulnerable, unaware state, it is much easier for entities to attack you in a variety of ways. Nighttime psychic attacks can take place either within your dreams while you are asleep, or you can be woken from sleep to experience the attack in a fully awake state. Both types of attacks can equally cause energetic, mental, emotional, and physical damage.

Do not write off an attack as your imagination if it occurs in your dreams. Psychic attacks during the dream state can be experienced as terrifying nightmares, sexual dreams, dreams of being chased or captured, or simply waking up with a horrible feeling of impending doom. Now, sometimes we do have the above dream experiences because our mind is working through some of our life stress while we sleep, but you should always keep in mind that it can most certainly be an indication of real psychic attack. Dreamtime psychic attack can also cause you to wake up in utter terror, covered in sweat, or freezing cold. During a dreamtime psychic attack, you may be having a nightmare due to your mind picking up on negative energy being sent your way by someone who wishes you ill intent. Your dreaming mind may be responding to actual spiritual entities attacking you on the mental plane. Or, if you are astral traveling during sleep (when your soul leaves your body and travels into the astral realm), you may be encountering malevolent entities in the astral realm.

Contrary to dreamtime psychic attacks, a physical psychic attack happens when you are fully awake. In this type of attack, there is an entity or some sort of spiritual phenomenon that is appearing to you, speaking to you, or outright attacking you physically. Oftentimes, people who experience this type of attack are awakened from a deep sleep only to realize there is something frightening happening in their room. In this type of attack, the victim may see or feel an entity in the room with them. Or, the figure may literally be on top of them. In some cases, the victim may be hit, pinched, tossed about, or even sexually assaulted by the dark being.

Some people will experience something called 'sleep paralysis,' in which they are completely unable to move, to defend themselves, or to call out for help. In many cases, the victim will be mentally aware during the attack, yet, the next thing they know, it is morning, and they do not remember what happened after the attack was through. This lapse in memory is called 'missing time.'

Whether the attack is in the dream state or in the physical realm, these types of attacks often revolve around an entity trying to feed off of the victim's life force energy, thus causing the person to experience extreme exhaustion or even illness after the attack. A 'night hag' is a grotesque-looking female spirit which sits upon the victim's chest while feeding off of his or her energy. In addition to the night hag, numerous spiritual beings like evil human spirits, demons, malevolent earth elementals, interdimensional beings, and many others (essentially any entity with negative intent) may choose to attack a person and feed off of their essence. There are also entities which specifically target sexual energy and feed off of it. The incubus and succubus, male and female demons respectively, can attack a person either in the dream state or in the waking state, their goal being to arouse sexual urges in the victim so they can feed off of the resultant energy.

Nighttime psychic attacks can happen to anyone regardless of age, gender, lifestyle, etc. Sadly, even children can be attacked, and may experience anything from a mild scare to a horrific brutal attack. For this reason, we must never ignore our children when they tell us they are experiencing scary things at night. Yes, some experiences are the result of an overactive childhood imagination, but some experiences are actual psychic attacks that require attention and intervention from the adults.

Many nighttime psychic attacks occur during one of two common time windows. The first is the midnight hour, also commonly called The Witching Hour, because, throughout history, this has been a popular time for magickal practitioners to cast their spells, curses, hexes, and so on. Anyone who is the unfortunate recipient of malevolent spell work may indeed experience symptoms of psychic attack at the midnight hour when the spell is being cast against them. The victim may experience a terrifying nightmare, suddenly feel overwhelmed with dread, or even see or sense negative energy or an entity in their bedroom. Another common time for psychic attack, especially entity attack, is between the hours of 3:00 a.m. and 4:00 a.m. It is said that the veil between the physical and spiritual worlds is thinnest at this time, making it easier for spiritual beings to manifest in the physical realm.

I would be remiss if I did not mention the fact that some people sleep during the day rather than nighttime. Those who work the night shift or who are night owls may regularly sleep during daylight hours. Everything I have described above can happen whether you are sleeping during the night or day, although, generally speaking, psychic attacks while sleeping tend to be more prevalent during the dark of the night. Regardless of when you sleep, it is important to take proactive steps for protection.

TIPS FOR PROTECTING YOURSELF FROM NIGHTTIME PSYCHIC ATTACKS

The biggest challenge to psychically protecting yourself while you're sleeping is that you are not able to be aware of your surroundings or actively protect yourself while you are asleep. Because of this, it is recommended that you take extra precautions during your sleeping hours. Below, I will list my favorite methods of psychic protection at night; however, this list is not exhaustive. I encourage you to use whatever works best for you.

Salt is my number one favorite protective nighttime tool. On a physical level, salt is highly absorbent, meaning it is exceptional at drawing things out. If you have ever gone swimming in the ocean, you may have noticed that your skin felt dry afterward. This is because the saltwater absorbed the moisture from your skin. You may have also taken baths with sea salt or Epsom salt, which are commonly used to draw toxins out of the body. Similarly, on a spiritual level, salt tends to absorb and dampen energy. A circle of salt has been used in many different traditions throughout history as a means of protecting the person inside the circle. Because salt can absorb energy, I choose to not use it 24 hours a day, but only when I am sleeping, dealing with a psychic attack, or doing a clearing on a person or home.

To use salt for nighttime psychic protection, you will first want to choose the salt that you feel most drawn to use. Simple table salt works just fine. As an alternative, you can also use coarse salt, sea salt, etc. Simply sprinkle salt around the perimeter of your bed. You can also sprinkle it under your pillow, between the sheets (if you don't mind sleeping on salt granules), or in the corners of your bedroom. Follow your inner guidance and use it as needed.

Another one of my other favorite nighttime protection

tips is to wear an amulet—a sacred or special object—around your neck. It can be a religious/spiritual icon, a gemstone pendant, a charm that has a sacred symbol etched on it, or anything that feels protective to you. On occasion, I have even slept with a rosary around my neck.

The use of frankincense essential oil is another go-to nighttime technique. Frankincense has long been used for sacred ceremony, protection, and even exorcism. You can purchase essential oils at your local organic grocery store although your results will be more powerful using higher-quality brands like Young Living and DoTerra. I like to put one drop of frankincense oil into my hand then dab a bit onto my crown chakra at the top of my head and anywhere else I feel I need it, as a way of anointing myself with powerful blessing and protection.

Lastly, you will want to make sure that your bedroom is a quiet, serene, sacred space, free of physical clutter and disruptive energies. I recommend removing all electronic devices, especially your television, computer, tablet, and cell phone, as these can disrupt your sleep and even have an adverse effect on your physical health. To ensure the best energy possible, make sure your bedding is clean and fresh and that your sheets and comforter are a design and color that feel good to you. Most importantly, fill your bedroom with objects that are sacred and protective to you—pictures, statues, knick-knacks, crystals, etc.—to enhance your space with the positive energy needed to ward off negative energies while you sleep.

CHAPTER 8 - AN ANGEL'S PROTECTION

Or was that the Demon Connection…
Immediately after my private session with Darlene, I felt safer and more uplifted. Darlene told me that I was now under her special angelic protection, and that gave me a lot of comfort. And yet, I was still noticing some disturbing things in my world.

A few hours after my session, I stopped off at Wal-Mart to pick up a few things. I was in happy spirits, thinking about how I was now fully protected and things would begin to get better for me. Before going in, I decided to do something different with my energy protection since I would often feel physically sick and energetically overwhelmed whenever I would go into a big chain store like this. Sitting in my car, I worked on strengthening my energy, and then set an intention that I would be in 'stealth' mode, that my energy would be invisible to any person or entity who intended harm. Feeling fully protected and light on my feet, I walked through the automatic doors and immediately heard the song, "Give Me a Higher Love," by Steve Winwood. My face lit up into a big smile and I felt my heart expand. As I walked through the clothing department, a female employee looked right at me and smiled with a mysterious look of knowing. I felt like I was surrounded by grace.

I continued with my shopping, and at one point I looked up and saw two young Caucasian men walking side-by-side, late-teens or early twenties, wearing blue jeans and t-shirts. I was walking down a main aisle with my cart, and they were in the process of coming out of a side aisle. In the split second it took to see them turn the corner, I immediately recognized that they were demonically possessed. Their eyes were completely black, and they looked directly at me with animosity as though I was their target. Once they turned the corner, they were walking right behind me and I knew I was in trouble. Intuitively, I knew they were going to try to place something harmful in my energy field on the back of my neck. Thinking quickly, I jerked my cart to the left and turned down the side aisle to get them off my back. Fingers crossed, I was pretty sure I had avoided whatever it was they had been trying to do to me.

After finishing my shopping at Wal-Mart, I went to the grocery store to pick up a few things. That was when I noticed that my neck was beginning to hurt. That night I woke up in the middle of the night to use the bathroom. As soon as I sat up in bed, I saw a scavenger demon watching me from my bedside table. It was small, less than a foot tall, gray and hairless. How did it get there? I thought I was protected!?

The next morning, my neck was killing me. After waking with a horrible crick in my neck, I went outside to do some grounding and meditation. My jaw dropped as I looked above my house to see demons flying in a circle above my roof. In past meditations, I had set up a grid of protection, a bubble of protective light, around the boundaries of my yard. The demons were circling right outside the dome of protection, several feet above my house, as though they were waiting for an opportunity to get through the barriers. I sat down on the grass for my morning meditation, and as soon as I cleared my mind, I intuitively saw a small demon attached to my back and neck and another one above my head. Through my intention, I tried to remove them. The one on my back dug in even deeper, and the one above my head hissed at me.

Crap! Why was this happening? I messaged Darlene about what was going on. We scheduled another private appointment and she agreed to teach me how to do energy combat. Wow, things were getting crazy!!! I was grateful to have someone who could help guide me.

After a couple of days of demons in and above my house and attached to my energy, I texted Darlene again to ask if she could do some long-distance healing work for me. I did not feel like I could wait until my next in-person session. She replied right away and said she would do some distant healing work for me and that she would follow up soon.

The next day, I had not heard from her, so I texted again. Maybe she was just really busy. No answer. The day after that, I texted again. Still no answer. Huh. I was going to be attending one of her group classes the following day, so I figured I could talk with her in person. Maybe after class she would even teach me about the spiritual combat she had mentioned before, so I could better protect myself.

The next day, I went to the group angel healing session led by Darlene. When I walked in the door, I saw her and made a beeline over to her to give her a hug. Oddly, her personality was much different than it had been before. Her personality seemed completely flat and expressionless. I wondered what was up. Previously, she had been friendly and happy to see me, but this time, she acted like she wanted to get away from me.

After class was over, I eagerly waited for the crowd to dissipate so I could talk with her privately. I gave her another big hug and thanked her for the class. We spoke softly so our conversation would be kept private.

"Maya," Darlene began, "I think you and I are going to be working together quite a lot now. I want you to feel free to schedule as many private sessions with me as you like. I know money is a concern for you, but do not worry about the cost of the sessions. We'll just work something out."

"Wow, thank you, Darlene! With everything going on, I haven't been able to focus on my business and income, so my finances have been in flux. Thank you for helping me. A while back, you mentioned that you would teach me spiritual combat so I can better protect myself. Can you teach me something now?" Darlene's face clouded over. "We really can't do that now since we're not in a private space. I'll teach you at your private session next Friday."

A feeling of despair shot through me. I had been going

through some really intense spiritual attack, and now I was going to have to wait nine more days. Ugh. But she was the boss, the expert.

"Okay," I said, feeling disappointed. "I'll see you at next week's appointment."

Over the next few days, things got even worse. I still was walking through my daily life with a demon burrowed into my back and neck and another one hovering above my head. In desperation, I texted Darlene again and asked if she could please do some long-distance healing work for me. She responded and said she would do it for me soon. After that, I didn't hear back from her.

I started really freaking out at this point! I needed *real* help, but she wasn't following through. I was feeling desperate and emotionally overwhelmed. Overcome with a feeling of complete existential crisis, I felt like I could barely function in my life. Late one night as I was dealing with all these feelings of overwhelm, I finally went to bed at 1:30 a.m. to try to get some rest. But I could not sleep. I was so upset that I could not figure out how to remove the demons that were attacking me. Every time I tried to remove them, they would dig in deeper.

I got up from bed and sat down at my computer. I typed in several different key phrases to try to find someone, anyone, who could help me. I recalled how I had reached out to my colleagues and my spiritual community and all I received in return was judgment and disbelief. Surely, there had to be someone who specialized in this type of work, someone who knew how to help me. I sat at that computer doing several searches for practitioners, support groups for entity attacks, or any resources that could help. The only thing I found was an organization in another state that has a months-long waiting list. How could this be? In my gut, I felt sure that I was not the only person in the world to experience demonic attack or serious psychic attack. Why were there no real resources, no support groups? It was at this moment that I decided that once I got through this (if I ever did!) I would create a support group to help others going through similar situations. I did not want anyone to have to go through this kind of living hell all alone.

I went back to my bedroom, sat on my bed, and sobbed. I prayed to God for some sort of sign, for something, anything! Apparently, I was supposed to figure out how to clear this stuff, but I had no clue how! I was feeling tons of frustration and lack of support. I picked a couple of angel cards, read their comforting messages, and began to calm down a bit.

Then, I suddenly noticed that a single bird began singing in my backyard. It was not the usual type of bird that commonly makes noise at night, like an owl or dove. The bird was singing a melody, but it did not sound like any bird I had ever heard before. As the bird sang, I listened intently. The birdsong sounded oddly artificial, and something seemed really off about it.

The next day, I had a long phone call with my friend

Sandra. She had recently had a phone session with Darlene and was telling me all about it. Sandra said that only five minutes into the phone call, Darlene had told her she thinks that both Sandra and her young daughter are part of the elite angelic crew who have a special mission for the world. I told Sandra that I was unsure about my own role, and that it feels suspect to me that Darlene would make that declaration to Sandra just five minutes into their call. I mean, if she is supposed to be helping us, why have I still been under attack? In fact, why have the attacks gotten significantly worse? Why have I not been protected, as Darlene said I would be?

Sandra shared, "Darlene told me that she is the 'mother' of this group of angels and that she is responsible for all of us. Maybe it's true. And maybe she hasn't been good about following up with you because she's really busy."

"I'm not sure what to believe." I replied, "I'm questioning everything right now. One thing I know for sure is that crazy stuff has been happening! And busy or not, if one of my own clients was being actively attacked by demons, I would take two seconds to text them back. The lack of follow-up feels professionally irresponsible to me. Something isn't right here. I can just feel it." I felt some anger welling up. I was going through a hellish experience, and I was getting pissed off! We both agreed that some things were not adding up, but we were unsure of what to believe.

The following weekend, I went to one of the X-Men

movies with my friend Raina and her boyfriend. They were both concerned about me with all I had been going through. The movie had a strong impact on me. Being a blockbuster superhero movie, the theme was all about the heroes using their powers to fight against the evil forces. The movie soundtrack was compelling, as was the storyline. After the movie was over, I felt inspired, stronger, and more empowered.

My friends and I parted company, and when I got into my car, there was a phone message from my birth father's wife. My birth father, Allen, had had some sort of mysterious health emergency. His legs had given out and he was mentally confused. The doctors said it was not a stroke, and in fact, that could not figure out what had happened to him. He was in the hospital and was awaiting further tests. I called his wife, Evelyn, right away, and after going over the details of what had happened, she said she would keep me posted with updates.

After hanging up the phone, my stomach sank. Not only was I deeply concerned about Allen, but I had a really bad feeling that it was connected to the severe psychic attack I had been experiencing. It was not uncommon for innocent family members, close friends, loved ones, even pets, to be directly attacked as a means to indirectly attack the primary target. I had no idea what I could do to help Allen and I prayed that his situation was not related to my psychic attack.

I drove home from the movie, deep in thought. As I stepped through my front door I heard a message loud and clear. "You must believe that you are strong...because you are." I realized that I should stay in the empowered energy of the movie I had just seen, so I went on iTunes and purchased the orchestral soundtrack to listen to over and over and keep myself in a more empowered state. After coming home from the movie, my back popped and much of the tension in my neck and back from the past week had suddenly released. It felt like the dark energy above my head was slowly dissolving, although still partially there.

A few days later, I still had not heard back from Darlene to help me with these spiritual warfare issues. I finally began to admit that I was growing angry with her. I thought about how at my last appointment with her, she had told me that I was under her full protection and I would not experience any further attacks. That was obviously false. I was feeling like she was a good person and full of information, but I realized I could no longer depend on her for psychic protection emergencies.

LESSON 8 – TAPPING INTO YOUR OWN PERSONAL POWER

The Dark Forces would like you to believe that you are not powerful; that you do not have the capability to protect yourself, and that these negative forces are stronger than you are. By initiating fear and disempowerment, they can gain control over their victim, while, in reality, much of this power is an illusion. The truth is that you are so much more powerful than you realize! Yes, it is prudent to have a healthy caution toward negative energies because they really can hurt you! But that should be balanced with a healthy connection with your own personal power, your ability to stand up for yourself and ward off situations that are not good for you.

The problem is, if you have had a lifetime of being a victim in your personal life, or if you have had ongoing issues with being the victim of psychic attack, you may not be feeling very empowered. Trying to tap into your inner power may feel much easier said than done! This is why tapping into your power is something that should be practiced on a daily basis. Like physical exercise, you will need to practice this regularly so you can strengthen your personal power muscles.

Recently, I asked a group of my students what they like to do to tap into their personal power in a way that gets them really pumped up. They gave me a lot of answers like meditation, being in nature, Reiki, relaxation breathing, gentle yoga, and relaxing. I was surprised by the responses. These are all techniques that can certainly help you get more calm, grounded, peaceful, balanced, and centered, and as such, yes, they do gently connect you with your power. But, if you are dealing with outright spiritual warfare, you are going to need something much stronger.

One benefit of gentle power is that it can be quite clear and focused; however, I would like to encourage you to connect that soft clarity with an even more powerful, fiery, passionate, earth-shaking energy. Do not be afraid of your energy. Many of you have been accustomed to keeping your personality and energy small so that you do not offend anyone or step on anyone's toes. But, if you are going to learn how to truly protect yourself from spiritual attack, you will need to tap into your inner power in a whole new way.

Depending on your personality, you may do best tapping into your power with inspiring activities, with physical movement, with focused meditation techniques, or a combination thereof.

First, I will give some pretty commonly known methods, then I will teach you some of my signature techniques.

Music:

Music is a fantastic tool for evoking strong emotional states of personal power. Depending on your musical preferences, you might reach for strong orchestral classical pieces like Beethoven's Fifth Symphony, Mozart's Symphony Number 25 in G Minor, or Vivaldi's Four Seasons. I am not normally drawn to listen to classical music in my everyday life, but I find that it has a timeless quality that inspires great intensity of feeling. You might also find music that really speaks to you in the modern popular music genres. Use what works for you. If it makes you feel powerful, use it.

One word of caution against heavy metal music. Now, I am not one of those people who says that heavy metal music is satanic, because lumping a whole genre of music as evil is simply ridiculous. I caution you to keep in mind that many who are energetically sensitive may find that heavy metal music lowers their vibration, thus making them more vulnerable to psychic attack. This is one musical style that tends to have a chaotic, angry energy to it. But here is the thing. Sometimes, we have been so disempowered that it is necessary to tune into anger as a means to find our personal power. If this is the case for you, chaotic, angry music may be best for you at this time. In the end, the goal is to eventually be able to tap into your inner power from a place of inspiration and love. Do what works for you.

Vigorous Physical Exercise:

Intense physical movement is one of the best ways to tap into your personal power. In the aftermath of experiencing the events in this book, I was desperately looking for ways to find a deeper level of power. I had been disempowered so long that mere meditation techniques were not cutting it for me. Intuitively, I knew that I would need to use my physical body to get the fires blazing. The next day, I called my local martial arts studio and signed up for classes. Even though I was probably the most remedial student in the class, I was not there to be the top student. I was there to find my inner fire.

Any intense physical activity can help you tap into your inner ferocity. Martial arts, kickboxing, running, and vigorous dancing can get your blood pumping and your power flowing. If you have a health condition that prohibits intense exercise, you can simply modify the movements, or choose a gentler form of exercise like Chi Gong, Tai Chi, or gentle yoga while holding the intention of activating your power.

Breathing:

Breathing is another powerful way to shift your energy. We all know that taking a few deep breaths can calm anxiety and feelings of being overwhelmed and help you to feel more clear and grounded. Taking deeper, intention-filled breaths for an extended period of time can enhance this effect even more. Sit in a chair with your spine straight and your feet flat on the floor. Start off by taking three slow deep breaths to get warmed up and grounded. Breathe in through your nose and out through your mouth, allowing your jaw to relax. Expand your belly out with each inhale and contract your belly on each exhale. Then, speed up your deep breathing so you inhale for two counts and exhale for two counts, inhaling deeply through your nose all the way down to your belly, then exhale by forcefully blowing out your mouth. Continue breathing two counts in, two counts out. Breathing forcefully like this will oxygenate your blood and make your body feel stronger. If you feel dizzy at any point, discontinue the deep breathing and begin breathing at your normal, natural pace for a while.

Expanding Your Aura:

In the aftermath of the intense psychic attack described in this book, one of my teachers, Holly, taught me this effective technique for taking charge of the energy around you. Sit in a chair with your spine straight and your feet flat on the floor. Take a few slow, deep breaths to help you become clear, centered, and grounded. After completing the grounding breaths, allow your breath to resume back to normal as you tune into your aura, the natural energy field surrounding your physical body. A normal, healthy human aura will usually extend about an arm's length beyond your physical body. With your intention, make your aura a little bigger and notice how that feels. Then, make your aura bigger and bigger until you fill the entire room and then your entire home and property. If you live in an apartment building, only expand your aura to the size of your apartment. If other people live with you, just modify accordingly. If it is your home, you have the right to expand your energy into the entire space. If you are not in your home environment, you might start off just expanding to fill your own personal space.

As you expand your energy, you are literally pushing out any energies and entities that do not belong. When I do this exercise, I always laugh a little because I imagine that I am forcefully belly bumping evil spirits out of my space. Those who are energetically sensitive may not feel well when performing this exercise. When you expand your aura, you also expand your energetic feelers, so to speak, so, if you are a sensitive empath, you will be picking up on a lot of information in your environment. Empath or not, I suggest trying this exercise and notice how it works for you. For some, this exercise will be a very effective way of taking charge of the energy around you. After all, you are the boss of your own energy and your own home. You have the right to take up all the space in your home and not let freeloading ghosts or negative entities in your space.

3-Part Energy Strengthening Technique:

This technique works much differently than the above aura expanding exercise because you are working not only with your own energy, but earth energy and universal energy as well. First, sit with your spine straight and your feet flat on the floor. Take a few slow, deep breaths to help you become centered and grounded. Next, focus on drawing energy up from the earth into the bottoms of your feet and your entire aura. You might imagine that this earth energy is a certain color, like deep green or a rich, earth brown. (I like using green because that color is an all-around healing vibration.) Allow this energy to fill up and empower your entire physical body and your entire aura. Once you feel complete with this, change your focus to the top of your head. Intend on calling in Divine energy from the Universe. If you wish, you can imagine that this Divine energy is a soft, pure golden light. Allow that energy to come in through the top of your head and the top of your aura, filling up both your physical body and your entire aura with this radiant, healing, protective Divine light. Take a nice deep breath. Now, place the palms of your hands on your heart chakra, the energy center in the middle of your chest. Feel and intend your heart energy getting bigger and bigger until it fills up your entire body and your entire aura. Your heart chakra is a beautiful, clear green emerald color. See and feel the color of your heart chakra radiating throughout your entire being. Now, how do you feel? This exercise is grounding, protective, and uplifting all at the same time.

CHAPTER 9 - A GLIMPSE OF TRUTH

I woke in the morning after a night of really crazy dreams. I wondered if perhaps I had been astral traveling because I felt like I had been visiting various different realms. In one astral journey, it seemed like I was in some type of underworld. I saw demons walking around, yet they were not aware of me. As I took in my surroundings, I noticed many colors in the environment that are different than what we see in our usual world. After I left that place, I had the sensation of flying over cliffs and oceans, soaring with freedom and exhilaration.

The next dream was more like a normal dream, not astral travel. I was in a mall and was inside a shop that sold makeup and did hair. I had gotten my long hair chopped off so it was short like Darlene's. I had not styled mine yet so it was just lying flat. I was going to get some styling product to give my hair some shape and texture but I had not done it yet. I had just bought some makeup and nail polish. (I am a natural gal, so I do not use any of that stuff in my real life.) I was looking at the products thinking, why did I buy this stuff? I would not normally put this on my skin because it is toxic! I walked out of the mall and realized I was in a parking lot with numerous malls. I had been in the wrong mall. I was walking around looking for Pine Tree Mall (the mall in my hometown) but I could not find it.

When I woke, I immediately wondered if the dream

had something to do with Darlene. While she had been informative, I really was not so sure about her anymore and whether I really wanted her as a mentor and teacher. Sandra and I had also been talking about how Darlene had told us that we are part of her elite group of angels, and that we were not sure if what she said was correct. Something was just not adding up. It was interesting how in the dream I was trying to be like her rather than just letting myself be who I am. I am usually someone who celebrates who I am, but I did understand that I had been giving some of my power away to Darlene. It was also fascinating that I dreamed I was in the wrong mall. Essentially, this meant that I had been seeking answers and guidance from the wrong place (Darlene), when I should have been seeking guidance from my own inner wisdom (my hometown mall).

I remembered back to my most recent one-on-one session with Darlene and how at one point out of the blue my throat felt like it was on fire. I mean, major pain comparable to a severe throat infection I had several years ago. When I told her about the sudden throat pain, she said that her angels were clearing my throat since I had been talking about being blocked with speaking my truth in the past. After about ten minutes, the pain reduced about 75%, and by the end of the day, 100%. Was that actual spiritual healing I had been receiving? Or, was it something else entirely?

And then I remembered another strange occurrence at that same appointment. As Darlene had been talking, something caught my eye about two feet to the left of her. I moved my gaze away from Darlene and saw a little girl, about twelve years old, with blonde ringlets and wearing a frilly pink satin dress with puffy sleeves. She was looking right at me, smiling sweetly. I was used to seeing spirits, so I just gave her a little smile and looked back to Darlene. Darlene looked a little puzzled when I did this. She did not ask what had happened and I did not feel called to share. As I thought back to this, I realized there had been something mildly creepy about the girl. She had been overly sweet looking, almost as though her candy-pink appearance had been a guise for something less than sweet.

By that point, Sandra, Raina, and I were talking on the phone and texting daily, often several times a day. In addition to Sandra, Raina, too, had recently connected with Darlene for a spiritual consultation. And now, all three of us were experiencing symptoms of psychic attack. Raina's mom was having mysterious health issues and the electronics in Raina's house and car were going haywire. Sandra was having really odd experiences — crows following her as she walked along the street, hearing voices in her house at night, demonic images showing up on her shower wall, and her young daughter was waking at night with nightmares.

Every day, Sandra, Raina, and I would take turns asking each other, "Am I crazy? Am I really experiencing this? Or is this just all in my head?"

"No, you're not crazy," we would affirm for each other. "You really are experiencing this!" There were so many times we would tell each other, "Oh my God, I don't know what I would do without you two!" We were all three going through something similar and it seemed to all be connected.

"Ladies," Raina said. "Have you considered that this might be an attack from a djinn?"

I countered, "I don't think that's what this is. You're talking about an evil genie, right? This seems to be mostly demonic-based, in my opinion." I did not know much about djinn and it was beyond the scope of my experience; however, I knew an awful lot about demons.

From Dream to Reality
One night, things got so weird that I was sure it would sound insane to anyone I would tell. I had a very fitful sleep, tossing and turning a lot and waking several times. At one point, I opened my eyes, sat up in bed, and saw Cookie Monster—yes, the blue furry Sesame Street character—standing in my bedroom. What the??? A few hours later, I woke again, sat up, and Batman was there. "Oh, come on!" I thought. "What the heck is this crazy stuff?"

When I woke in the morning, I opened my eyes and clearly saw a man, with a muscular bare chest, holding a large sword in one hand and kneeling down on one knee. He seemed to be making a gesture that he was at my service as a protector. The first thing I thought of was Archangel Michael. But then, I realized something did not feel right. His wings were folded into his back so I could not see them. I had seen Archangel Michael on several occasions, but never with his wings hidden like that. Somehow, I had this knowing that he was keeping his wings hidden because they were not white angel wings but were the black wings of a demon. At that moment, I realized that I was being tricked to think this was Archangel Michael when it was something else entirely.

Then, I remembered how I had seen Cookie Monster and Batman during the night. My mind was trying to figure this out. I had never had any type of experience with mental health hallucinations and did not have any history of mental illness. Was the being that was causing the overall psychic attack trying to confuse me and make me question my sanity? Was all of this just a figment of my imagination? But then, I thought of example after example of times in the past when I had seen things clairvoyantly or otherwise received information psychically, and my experiences had been validated again and again by other people! The visions I had of Cookie Monster, Batman, and the false angel all felt just like the hundreds of other valid clairvoyant experiences I had experienced in the past. Over time, I had learned to believe and trust what I see, hear, and feel is true and valid. But what on earth was going on with these recent visions? Obviously, I knew that Cookie Monster and Batman are fictional television characters.

I got up and went about my usual morning routine, unrolling my yoga mat and doing some gentle stretching. My body was tense from all that had been happening, so I tried to breathe deeply. Maybe this (daily constant psychic attack) would be my new normal. A pang of fear shot through my heart as I considered that maybe this issue would be with me for the rest of my life. What if I never got rid of whatever was attacking me? I took some more slow deep breaths and did some more stretching, trying to encourage a calmer state.

After thirty minutes, I was indeed in a more peaceful state, much more grounded. As I stood up to roll up my yoga mat, I happened to glance at Darlene's angel book that was resting on the table. I had been reading the book right before bed the evening before and had left it on the living room table. Because I had just finished a yoga session, my mind was relaxed and my intuition was open. In that open, calm, intuitive state, I suddenly saw the book cover in a whole new light. The book cover has a picture of an angel with large white wings in a blue sky with clouds. The angel is holding an opalescent crystal. As I gazed at the stone on the book cover, I suddenly realized I was looking at the image of a demon face, hiding in plain sight! Oh my God! What?! Then, I looked even more closely at the crystal, and in the center, what I believe was meant to illustrate light reflecting, there was a white area that looked just like an evil eye, with a vague resemblance to the Eye of Sorin from the Lord of the Rings Trilogy. A chill went down my spine.

Sandra had had an experience a few months ago with a jealous friend who had given her a handmade painting of peacock feathers, and the design on the feathers had looked like eyes watching her. Eventually, she had to destroy the painting when she realized it was giving her jealous friend direct access to psychically attack and keep intuitive surveillance on her. If not for Sandra's recent experience, I may not have put two and two together when I saw the eye on Darlene's book cover.

Upon closer inspection, I found numerous demon faces on the opalescent surface of the crystal, as well as within the clouds. They were literally all over the book cover, nearly thirty demon faces hidden in plain sight on a book cover that was supposed to be about angels. My mind was reeling.

I called Sandra immediately. (Raina was at work.) I told her about the events from the night before and the crazy things I had seen, as well as what I had just seen on the book cover. I took a picture of the book cover with my phone camera and texted it to her.

"Oh my God, Maya!" Sandra exclaimed. "I do see tons of demons on this book cover!"

My mind still could not quite untangle exactly what was going on, so I decided to recount the entire story with her step by step, from when I encountered Darlene at a local healing event, how the psychic attacks began, and how everything had unfolded. As I went through everything step by step, the veil was lifting and I was beginning to see the truth. I had not had any issues with entity/demonic attacks like this until I had begun working with Darlene, and as soon as I had purchased her pin and book, the attacks had gone through the roof. I had even brought her pin into my bedroom for protection while I slept. The pin is the same design as the book cover, with large angel wings and the opalescent stone in the center. Less than forty-eight hours after pinning that angel on my bedside lampshade, I had the first demonic attack, and from there, it got worse and worse! As I recounted the story to Sandra, I also realized that the night I returned home from the event with Darlene, it had been a full moon.

I kept repeating to Sandra, "But, Darlene is such a nice person! I can't understand why there are demons on her book! That doesn't make sense to me!" Sandra and I tried to sort it out. Was there some type of negative influence from whomever had designed her angel pin and her book? Or was the negative influence from Darlene herself? But, then I would go back into my loop of "But, Darlene is such a nice, lovely person! I can't believe she would intentionally work with demonic forces!"

Sandra finally interrupted me, "Well, even though we don't have all the answers yet, I do think you should remove the pin and the book as soon as possible. As an experiment, see what happens once you've gotten them out of your house."

As we talked on the phone, I took the angel pin and the book, wrapped them both in cloth, put them in a box, drew Reiki symbols, placed the box in the far corner of my garage with a cloth over it, and then cleansed my whole house with sage. "There," I said to Sandra, "We'll see if that makes a difference."

We rehashed the chain of events over a ninety-minute phone call. As we talked it out, everything was becoming clearer and clearer and a new understanding was flowing into me. I saw how I had pinned the angel on my lampshade and how the pin had served as a surveillance device (imagine an eye watching you), and as a portal, establishing direct access for any spiritual attack from Darlene (or whatever entities she works with). I was very sure that whatever Darlene was working with, it was most certainly not angels.

Sandra and I went in circles, asking, "But does Darlene know she's not working with angels? Does she know her so-called angels are imposters—demons disguised as angels? Is she doing this intentionally? Or is she being fooled?" Despite my recent frustration with Darlene's unhelpfulness during my psychic attack, I had always liked her and even felt a sisterly affection toward her. I was having a hard time believing that she would intentionally be working with Dark Forces, yet, at this point, I really did not know what to believe.

After I got off the phone with Sandra, I checked my energy field and was amazed that there were no demons to be found. I checked through my home, and all was clear there, too. There was absolutely no sign whatsoever of entity activity or psychic attack.

After thirty-six hours of no further attacks, I began to think about an acquaintance, Crystal, who was mentoring closely with Darlene. Crystal, a very sweet and sincere young woman, had been under severe demonic attack for a few years now, and, according to Crystal, Darlene had been helping her through those attacks. "I would probably be dead today if not for Darlene's help," Crystal had told me a few months back. As I thought about my own situation, about Sandra and Raina, and about Crystal, I wondered if Darlene did not actually help people experiencing psychic attack, but rather, she (or whatever entity is working through her) was the one who was actually causing the attacks. I began to feel very concerned about Crystal so, that evening, I sent her a text.

"Hi, Crystal. I am concerned about some things. Please be very careful with trusting those around you, especially your teachers. And please use caution with any jewelry you may have gotten from them." Ethically, I did not feel I should get specific with names, but still, I was worried about her and felt I should warn her.

LESSON 9 – UNDERSTANDING AND RECOGNIZING ENERGY PORTALS

Understanding and recognizing energy portals is a vital aspect of proper energy protection. In reality, you could be doing the best energy clearing possible for yourself and your home, but if there are portals present, it will be like trying to scoop water out of your endlessly leaky boat. In this section, I will teach you what energy portals are, how to identify them, and how to close them.

What Are Energy Portals?

An energy portal is a doorway, an energetic opening, where energies and entities can pass through from other locations, other times, even from other dimensions. Similar to what science calls a 'wormhole,' a passage through space time which creates shortcuts from one place to another, an energy portal creates a passageway for paranormal activity to pass through, allowing entities to come and go. Essentially any type of being can pass through an energy portal, from angels and light beings, to deceased loved ones, ghosts, earth elementals, evil spirits, demons, and more. A portal can be present in a physical object (like the stone in my angel pin), in a mirror, a piece of furniture, or a wall hanging. They can also be present in the structure of a building, like a wall, ceiling, floor, or even simply in mid-air. Portals can exist not only in connection with physical objects or building structures, but also in nature. I once saw two tree branches that formed into the shape of a small, oval doorway and I immediately recognized it as an opening where fairy-folk pass through. Portals can also form in natural environments. Ley lines, the natural alignment of Earth energies, can create a portal or energy vortex in an area.

How Are Energy Portals Formed?

Homes and buildings which have had ongoing negative energy, traumatic events, excessive suffering, death, murder, tragedy, or dark spiritual practices are common places where portals may form. A toxic workplace, a home with domestic violence or drug use, a hospital or morgue, a location where black magick is being performed, a murder crime scene, a prison, a concentration camp, these are all examples of locations that might develop one or more energy portals, not to mention general paranormal activity as well. From my observation, it is primarily mischievous or malevolent entities that pass through portals created through negative events, while angels and light beings tend to pass through portals at holy places like churches, temples, and sacred groves. Keep in mind that any type of entity can pass through any type of portal, no matter how it was formed.

Objects can serve as portals when they are charged, intentionally or unintentionally, with negative energy or negative intent. For example, someone working with conscious malevolent intent may 'program' an object to become a portal, then pass the object along to their intended victim so they can have a direct passageway to psychically attack them. Examples of this would be the angel pin sold to me by someone working on behalf of the Dark Forces, as well as the peacock painting given to my friend Sandra by a jealous friend.

Some objects are not intentionally turned into portals, but rather, these are objects that have unintentionally received negative energy from people, locations, or situations, such as an armoire that was in the home of a chronically hateful, toxic person; a mirror that was in a bar where a murder took place; a ring worn by someone practicing black magick; etc. In other words, the portal was not created intentionally, but was instead created by default due to the low vibration energy to which it was exposed.

Some objects are more likely to become portals than others. Antique objects and furniture can hold the long history of prior owners. Metal tends to hold onto energy (whether positive or malevolent) much more readily than wooden objects or cotton fabric. Metal conducts energy and can strengthen the power of a spiritual entity. In addition, you can assume that nearly all mirrors are portals by default no matter what kind of energy they are exposed to. Mirrors are natural doorways to the spirit realm. Lastly, wall hangings, tapestries, and personal items that are in a mandala pattern (an intricate, round geometrical shape) can often become portals because they focus and intensify energy in a particular way. The effect reminds me of the wormhole in the 1994 movie, Stargate.

Ouija boards, also called spirit boards, are used as a divination tool to talk with spirits. The problem arises due to the fact that the Ouija board also acts as a doorway for spirits to pass through and communicate with the people using the board, thus making it a portal.

Can Humans Be Portals?

Absolutely. Humans themselves can be portals, although this is somewhat rare. Some people have a particular quality to their energy which creates a sort of portal through which entities can come and go. This can occur because of past trauma, karma, a soul contract, or it can even be passed down generationally.

What's the Difference?

We should take a moment here to distinguish the difference between a portal, an object that is cursed, and a location that is haunted. A portal is a specific type of phenomenon where a spiritual doorway is established, allowing entities and energies to pass through. A cursed object is a physical item that can create bad luck for the owner, but it is not necessarily acting as a portal. A haunted location is a place where one or more spirits are actively present, making themselves visible, making noises, moving objects, etc.; however, a portal may or may not be present at a haunted location.

A Portal Is a Portal

Many people assume that positive portals created with

sacred intent will always be beneficial. This could not be further from the truth. A portal is a portal. If you are having issues with unwanted paranormal activity in your home, I recommend that you remove all portals until your issue is completely resolved. Even if the object matches your decor perfectly and you love it so much, if it's a portal, it's a portal. It does not matter how much you love it.

Beloved to many, the Native American medicine wheel used for sacred ceremonies is actually a portal used to call in spirits from the five directions. Native American dreamcatchers, which are said to keep away nightmares, are also portals. Bad dreams travel from the person's bedroom, through the dreamcatcher to the spirit world where they will no longer bother the dreamer. The problem is, once these portals are open, it is possible for spirits of any kind to pass through. I have a special place in my heart for both the sacred medicine wheel and dreamcatchers, but if you are experiencing unwanted paranormal activity, you are going to have to hide your dreamcatchers away for a while and dismantle your medicine wheel until things are clear.

Crystal grids are a popular practice in today's New Age culture as a means of focusing and enhancing energy for a specific purpose. To make a crystal grid, select crystals that will enhance your intention and place them in a geometric formation, like a circle, hexagon, star, etc. We will not be going into the details of crystal grids here except to say that, yes, a crystal grid is a portal because it creates a doorway for energy to pass through. Like medicine wheels and dream catchers, crystal grids are positive and uplifting; nevertheless, they are portals. If you are experiencing unwanted paranormal activity, you will need to put your crystals away until the issue is resolved.

3 Steps to Clear and Close Portals

The most effective way to take care of a portal problem is to completely remove the objects. If you are willing to part from these objects forever, take them to some abandoned land and bury them face down in the earth. Some people recommend burning problematic objects, but I discourage this. Quite often, burning an object actually releases the negative energy into the surrounding area rather than neutralizing the energy, and since fire can act as an amplifier, this release of negative energy can be quite powerful.

If you do not want to completely get rid of your items, you can wrap them in a silk or cotton cloth, place them in a box, and remove them from your home until your unwanted paranormal activities are completely resolved. When you are ready, you can bring these items back. If any paranormal activity starts up again, you may need to consider getting rid of the items altogether.

Larger items like mirrors and furniture cannot so easily be removed, and it would be inconvenient to do so temporarily. In this case, try covering the item with a large bedsheet or plain cloth until the unruly spiritual activity subsides. Cotton and silk fabrics are fairly effective at dampening energy. If the problem still persists, however, you may have to make arrangements to remove the item for good. Think twice before giving these items to charity, because you will likely be passing the portal issues onto the new owners. Unfortunately, the object may need to go to the landfill.

Lastly, if you are dealing with an object that you simply cannot bear to part with or cover up, you can try clearing and closing the portal. There are several methods for clearing objects: covering the object in salt, immersing in salt water, placing in the sun or moonlight, temporarily burying the object in the earth, holding under running water, doing Reiki, saying prayers, burning sage, and more.

Once you have cleared the energy of the object, you will want to then close the portal. You can do this by saying a prayer for protection, calling in Archangel Michael to close this portal now and forever. Next, call on the angel guardians for that home, building, or location, and ask them to stand guard, making sure this portal remains closed and that nothing is allowed to pass through. If you are a Reiki practitioner, you might also draw the power symbol over the portal, repeating the name of the symbol, stating, "This portal is now closed, now and forever." Similarly, if you have another spiritual practice which uses symbols of protection, you may use one or more of those symbols to close your portal.

If you are dealing with a portal that is within the

structure of the building or in nature itself, you will follow the process above by choosing a clearing technique (like prayers or Reiki), then calling in Archangel Michael and the angel guardians or using symbols to close the portal.

At this point, if you are still having issues, you may have to call on the assistance of a professional who does on-site or long-distance house clearings.

CHAPTER 10 - THE ANGEL OF WRATH

Not Again

It was 3:00 in the morning when I was violently jolted awake. My eyes flew open. A few feet above me was a blob of energy that looked like hot, pulsating, electric white light. Lightning fast, the entity reached into my body, grabbed my soul, and in one violent movement, tried to yank it out of my body.

I gasped, then blinked in utter shock. The entity, which had looked like a formless blob just moments ago, seemed to be vaguely taking on the form of an angel. Still somewhat formless, there was the impression of wings extending out from either side of the plasma-like being. "Is this an angel?" I thought.

Suddenly, I became completely aware of emotions and thoughts coming from the entity. Wrath. There were waves of it coming from the being. Without actually hearing any sound, I received a message so loud and clear into my being, it was undeniable.

"Don't mess with her. She's mine!" It was like the message had been directly seared into my brain.

Terrified out of my mind, I turned onto my side, covered my head with my arms, sobbing and hyperventilating uncontrollably for hours until the sun came up. I was afraid the entity would try to kill me. I was too scared to sleep, and too scared to move.

Finally, after sunrise I got up and walked with wobbly legs to the bathroom to splash cool water on my eyes. I grabbed my phone and texted Raina and Sandra a long, panicky message. Even though it was really early in the morning, Raina called me to make sure I was okay. I could not stop crying and she could barely understand what I was saying. Finally, I calmed down enough to explain what had happened.

"Are you okay?" she asked. "Do you think it's around you now?"

"I don't know. I don't think so." With a shaky voice, I talked in circles, "Was this actually an angel? If this was an angel, it was unlike any I've ever encountered! It was wrathful and terrifying. That was not a loving energy! Do angels attack people like that? Is Darlene working with some sort of wrathful angel? If that's true, what does this say about angels? Or is she working with some other kind of entity?"

I started to cry again, feeling confused and overwhelmed as I tried to understand what had happened. "And what did it mean when it said, 'Don't mess with her. She's mine.'? Who was it talking about? Darlene? Or Crystal? Or someone else? Was it the entity that's working through Darlene, and it was angry that I was warning people about the truth about her? Or was Darlene's entity angry that I had warned her number one student, Crystal? Or was it something attached to Crystal? Ugh, I don't know!"

My head hurt. As I recounted the story to Raina, I was

sure about one thing. There had been absolutely no entity activity for thirty-six hours after removing Darlene's book and angel pin from my home. And just a few hours after sending Crystal a warning text yesterday evening, I had been violently attacked by a wrathful, angry dark being.

"Raina, I have a one-on-one appointment with Darlene tomorrow morning, but I am scared shitless! If that attack happened with her accessing me long distance, what could happen in person?!"

Even though the past demonic attacks had been scary, they had not scared me nearly as much as this! What the f***! And seriously, out of *any* of the experiences I have had so far in this cycle of psychic attack, this was by far the most real and the most jarring.

"Should I cancel my appointment and immediately discontinue all further contact with her? Or face her? Holy shit!"

Ultimately, I decided to cancel and have no further contact with Darlene. I texted her, stating that something had come up, and that I needed to cancel. Normally, I would be more straightforward and explain my reason, but in this case, I felt that could put my safety at risk.

Interestingly, even though she had been so unresponsive through my emergencies, in this instance, she replied within minutes. She seemed unaware that anything was wrong and suggested some methods of rescheduling. I did not reply at all.

An hour or so later, with no reply from me, she texted again. "Hi Maya. I'm sorry the past couple of weeks have been so hard on you." And she sent another similar text about an hour after that. Then, later in the afternoon, she sent a Facebook message saying she was concerned about me and offering to drive out to my place on Sunday for a face-to-face session (a forty-minute drive for her). I did not reply to any of it. I was being extremely cautious about my safety.

I texted Raina and Sandra and updated them on my cancelling with Darlene and how she had suddenly been so responsive. They both texted back, each saying that Darlene had messaged them both quite early that morning, before I had even contacted them about my recent violent attack. They both thought it was very interesting timing that she would reach out to connect with them because she had been so unconcerned with following up with each of them in the past.

The next day, Darlene called and left me a voicemail. "Hi Maya. It's Darlene. Hey, hon, I really wanted to try to connect with you. I feel like I have failed you, I guess, over the past couple of weeks to show up in a way that you needed me to. I wanted you to know that whenever I would tune into you, my angel would tell me not to follow up with you. Also, I think I got pretty overwhelmed with people that were coming in with needs and it's not really an excuse. I deeply care about you. I hope you're doing well. I'd just like an opportunity to chat with you and check in. It's been a strange couple of weeks and I was hoping we could compare notes as well. But anyway, give me a call when you can. I appreciate it. Thanks. Bye."

I am normally someone who will take the opportunity to communicate whenever possible, especially as a means to clear up any misunderstandings. Honestly, if it had not been for the most recent violent attack, I most likely would have replied to her messages. But it was clear to me that she had only been trying so hard to get in touch with me because she was losing her grip on me (and my friends). She was trying to re-engage any way she could. No way was I going to let her plug back into me!

The violent entity attack had shaken me to my very core. After sunrise, I had packed some of my things and headed out to Lake Pontchartrain for several hours. I brought numerous books on psychic self-defense, angels, demons, and more. I also brought my tablet computer and was doing research online. I was in hyper-vigilant mode but was trying to ground.

In the late afternoon, on a whim, I messaged Holly, one of my business and intuition mentors, to tell her about the prior night's event. She had been a professional ghost hunter and has loads of knowledge in all things paranormal. She replied back immediately and we had an in-depth online discussion.

Holly explained that we are dealing with a very nasty type of entity called a djinn. The funny thing is, Raina had suggested this early on, but it had not clicked for me. I did not know what djinn were, had never heard of them, and therefore, did not believe in them. But the more Holly explained, the more I realized that perhaps Raina had been right all along.

The djinn are entities that operate by creating huge amounts of drama and confusion. They are made of flameless fire — plasma — and they are shape-shifters that can shift into animals, elementals, demons, angels, and more. Djinn can even manipulate reality and bend time to try to make someone think they are crazy.

"Wow, this all fits," I thought. Both Sandra and I had noticed animals, especially birds, acting strangely. I saw elementals and fairies the morning after acquiring the angel pin, not to mention seeing multiple demons. And most recently, the entity I saw looked like plasma trying to take the form of an angel. The weeks-long psychic attack had included strange bends in reality and time. Then, I recalled the bird I had heard singing in the middle of the night a few weeks back, singing an eerie song I had never heard before and have not heard since. It was the oddest, most disjointed birdsong, almost as though something was pretending to be a bird but did not know how to do the birdsong correctly. I thought about my experience with missing time, about seeing images of Cookie Monster and Batman, of wondering if I was losing my mind. And all the other crazy details!

Even though I was still deeply shaken up about the violent psychic attack I had experienced the night before, I felt better now having a clue as to what had been going on. Holly explained that I had made a mistake in not completely disposing of the book and angel pin, and that it was these items that had allowed the recent violent attack. Her suggestion was to burn them both and then bury the ashes far away. We also discussed the most effective methods for using herbs and tree resins to clear out serious attacks. I packed up my bag of books, ready to go home and take some empowered action for my own psychic self-defense.

LESSON 10 – BURNING TREE RESINS FOR PSYCHIC PROTECTION

In this section, I will be teaching you how to do exorcism-strength energy clearing. We will be using plant resins — dried tree sap — which is burned as incense. There are various resins that can be utilized for exorcism. For simplicity's sake, I will focus on the most common and widely used — frankincense resin.

The popular practice of the burning of sage is often believed to clear out everything, including really powerful, malevolent entities. The truth is, most of the time, sage is not effective in clearing out the really nasty stuff. In fact, in my own experience, evil spirits basically just laugh when we try to burn sage to clear them out because it is so ineffective. Now, the exception is when someone believes so deeply in the power of sage, and is using their own really powerful intention, and their inner power is so strong, that they are able to get that evil entity to leave.

To clarify, it is not the sage that is causing the clearing. It is actually the person's focused intent and will, and belief in the sage. It is the person's own energy that is forcing the negative being to leave. I have had people argue angrily with me over this point because they have such a strong emotional attachment to sage. Don't get me wrong. I love sage, and in fact, I use it nearly every day. Sage is a lovely tool for blessing and consecrating, as well as clearing out minor negative energies from everyday living. But, just because sage is popular and beloved by many does not mean it will work effectively in exorcising evil spirits.

Now, the difference is tremendous between burning sage compared to burning raw tree resins. Unlike sage, these tree resins are extremely effective in exorcising evil spirits. No matter the power or expertise of the person doing the clearing, the dried tree sap of frankincense has innate exorcism powers in and of itself. The vibration of the plant energy is what helps to clear negative vibrations. It is no surprise that the infant Jesus was gifted with frankincense, and that the Catholic Church has traditionally used billowing clouds of frankincense incense during Holy Mass. Frankincense is extremely effective in casting out evil spirits.

With this technique, you will be burning tree resins to produce a powerful, aromatic incense. But, let me be clear; we are not burning standard incense sticks, as these are commonly produced with synthetic materials that do nothing to clear out negative energies. If you want to achieve actual results, you will need to obtain real tree resins. The dried tree sap usually looks like little pebbles, although some brands will sell pieces that are in bigger chunks. You can acquire your supplies from either a reputable online store or your local metaphysical store. When shopping online, you will want to do your search using a phrase like "raw frankincense resin."

In addition to the frankincense resin, you will also need a fire safe bowl, incense charcoal, sand, and a small spoon and tongs. Many people like to use an abalone shell for burning sage as well as resins; however, keep in mind that the bowl will get extremely hot when you burn resins on a hot coal. I prefer using a soapstone incense burner bowl since it does not get nearly as hot as other bowls. Online, you can do a search for "soapstone incense burner bowl" and find many options. Be aware of the temperature of your vessel and have a potholder to handle your hot bowl.

The incense charcoal is a special type of charcoal that is used for incense and hookah pipes, and is not to be confused with the toxic charcoal used to cook food on a grill. Incense charcoal is a flat, round disc with slightly raised sides to create a bowl-like effect which keeps the resin from spilling off. You will also need sand (or salt) to put in the bottom of the dish underneath the charcoal. Some people use regular sand you could acquire from a garden shop, while most people use white sand which can be found by typing "white sand for burning incense" into the internet search bar. Lastly, you will need a small spoon and tongs. Both of these can be acquired from any shop that sells metaphysical items. Or, you can find them online by typing in "incense burning spoon tongs." You could also use a small teaspoon and a set of small kitchen tongs. If you are on a budget and want to start small, try searching online for "incense burning kit" and you will find an inexpensive kit that has a little bit of everything.

Supplies List:

- Raw tree resin (Choose from frankincense, myrrh, or dragon's blood. Use your intuition to choose, or, if you are not sure, simply start with frankincense.)
- Fire safe bowl
- Incense burning charcoal
- White sand (or salt) for incense burning
- Small spoon and tongs
- Lighter

Instructions:

1. Fill the bottom of your fire safe bowl with sand.
2. Holding your charcoal with tongs, light one edge of the charcoal until that edge begins to glow red. Then, blow on the charcoal three or four times to increase the glow. Set the charcoal lightly onto the sand to allow it more time to heat up.
3. Keep an eye on the charcoal, and in about five to ten minutes, the whole charcoal should be glowing red when you blow on it. If it seems slow to heat up, you can blow on it a bit more, being careful to not blow so hard that you cause sand or charcoal sparks to blow back at you.
4. When the charcoal is fully lit, spoon a bit of incense onto the charcoal. You will want to make

sure you do not cover the whole charcoal with incense because it needs oxygen to stay lit. Simply sprinkle some resin into the middle of the charcoal. Use enough incense to create a lot of smoke. The idea here is to create as much smoke as possible, as this allows the incense to do its job of clearing. You may choose to open the front and back doors and even some windows as a symbolic way of allowing the negative energy to leave. However, the clearing will work just fine, whether the doors and windows are open or not.

5. Use a potholder to pick up your fire safe bowl, allowing the smoke to billow as you walk to the front of the house. Start by clearing the area surrounding the front door, simply allowing the smoke to permeate that whole area. Continue with that room and any other rooms in the front of the house, gradually moving to the back of the house. If your home has an attached garage, carry your incense into the garage to clear that entire space. Work your way to any upper floors, following your inner guidance on which rooms to do first. If your home has a basement, it should be cleared last, allowing the smoke to infuse the whole foundation of the structure. As you go from room to room, don't forget areas like closets, pantries, etc. Depending on the severity of your paranormal issues and where

they have been taking place, you may also want to do this process outside in your yard, as well as inside your exterior garage or shed. This is my own preferred order of clearing a house; however, there really is no right or wrong way. In fact, I usually do it different each time, based on how I am intuitively guided. I encourage you to also follow your own inner guidance on this.

6. As you are going from room to room, it is likely that the incense will burn out, so you will need to add more incense to your charcoal. One charcoal disc should be sufficient for a small to average-size house. If you are clearing a large house or building, you may have to start a second charcoal and do the clearing in segments.

7. You may choose to add prayers, incantations, or blessings spoken aloud as you do this clearing process, but know that the incense in and of itself is powerful enough to exorcise spirits all on its own.

8. I like spending extra time in the bedrooms because you want to provide the most protection possible for the people who sleep in those rooms. Allow the smoke to completely fill each bedroom. Allow enough time before sleeping for the smoke to settle and for the air to clear.

A few more details….

Even though the plant resins are all-natural, animals can be affected by the thick smoke. If your animal is sensitive, you might consider removing them temporarily while you do the clearing. My two cats have always remained present during many, many clearings and they have always been fine. Nonetheless, you can never be too careful. Also, be aware that all this smoke can make your smoke detectors go off.

If you are experiencing unwanted paranormal activity in your home, it will not be enough to do this process just once. For serious issues, you will need to burn incense once a day, preferably at night for extra protection while you and your loved ones sleep. For extreme situations, you may need to do this twice a day, morning and night, or even have a bit of incense burning constantly throughout the day. For occasional issues that are not too serious, burning incense every two to three days may be enough. And for those not having serious issues, a once-a-week clearing will usually be sufficient to keep the space clean and clear.

How it works:

The incense smoke works a lot like a bug bomb or mosquito repellant. I know this might sound gross, but let's pretend you have a major flea infestation in your home. You would not do just one treatment and hope for the best. No, if you did that, the bugs would come back even worse than before! In order to totally get rid of the infestation, you would need to do regular eradication, remedy anything in your house that is bringing in the fleas, wash everything in your house again and again, and do even more bug bombs until the problem goes away for good.

In a similar manner, spirits hate the smoke of these tree resins. In most cases, the entities will move out of your house in order to avoid the smoke. In my personal experience, they will stay out for about three days, for as long as it takes for the energy of the plant resins to dissipate. Then, these spirits will often come right back in. This is why you will need to do this practice again and again, without waiting too long between each time. Don't get lazy about it simply because it seems like all is clear. In most cases, you will regret it. Be diligent about clearing every day and keep doing it for a few weeks after the problem seems to have resolved. It is best to do too much rather than not enough. Eventually, the spirits will find your space inhospitable and they will seek out a location that is more to their liking, leaving you alone at last.

Keep in mind that they might come back in the future if something triggers them to do so. But not to worry — you now have the tools to clear them out again. Once you learn to recognize even the hint of paranormal activity beginning to start, you will be able to nip it in the bud right away, helping to avoid a problem before it even begins. My mentor, Holly, explained the bug bomb analogy to me, and I have passed this description on to many of my clients and students.

There are a variety of techniques that can be used to drive out evil entities; however, this technique is the simplest and the most direct, and literally anyone of any experience level can perform it. Fluffy techniques like imagining love and light and calling in angels unfortunately do not work 99% of the time, whereas, a physical technique such as burning frankincense works quite effectively most of the time. Personally, I love working with angels and light, but when I am encountering major spiritual warfare, I also use my tools which have been proven effective again and again. So, feel free to use any techniques that call to you, but be sure to include burning frankincense into your arsenal of defense.

CHAPTER 11 - PARANORMAL ACTIVITY

Ring of Fire

It was a warm June day when I gathered my lighter wand and old newspapers and headed outside to start a fire in my fire pit. As I gathered sticks for kindling, I pondered all that had been happening over the past several weeks. I was eager for it all to be done with for good! I went into my garage and found the cardboard box where the angel book and pin had been stored away, wrapped carefully in a cloth. Unwrapping them, I felt a chill go down my spine. Holding the lighter, I lit the newspapers in the fire pit with prayerful intention and watched the kindling quickly catch fire. I threw more sticks onto the pile, allowing the fire to strengthen and grow. Having been raised Catholic, I naturally fell back to the traditions of my past and began reciting the Our Father and Hail Mary aloud, praying for protection and safety.

I took a deep breath and tossed the book then the pin into the fire. The flames shot up with alarming ferocity and I gasped. I continued my prayers as I stoked the fire, watching the pages of the book shrink and curl up like dried leaves. I was surprised to see the metal pin melt so easily in the fire as I continued to recite prayers with conviction. The fire was unusually hot and was unlike any campfire I had ever seen. In hindsight, I realize that it was ill-advised to burn the objects. (Instead, I should have buried the objects face down out in the middle of nowhere.) It was clear that the evil energy of the objects was being unleashed through the fire. As I gazed at the flames, I could see the faces of demonic entities, reminding me of the fires of Hell. I kept praying and stoking the fire. When the objects had fully burned and the fire had died down to embers, I sat down on the grass and breathed a huge sigh of relief. Hopefully, burning the objects would eradicate the entity issue once and for all.

Later that afternoon, I was sitting outside under a tree with my computer doing some administrative work on my energy healing business. I was feeling hopeful. I had just burned the cursed items and now I could move on and leave all this drama behind me. Although I was feeling a bit shaky, I was trying to forge ahead and get back to my usual life.

My computer dinged, indicating that someone had just sent me a private message on Facebook. It was from my friend Debbie. I opened the message and my hopeful heart sank and felt like it was being crushed. I had not even finished reading the entire message before I was sobbing loudly. All the pain I had been holding in over the past few weeks came pouring out in one big flood. I had been doing an okay job holding myself together through the recent terrifying events, but that message was the final straw that pushed me over the edge. She had been one of the few people I had confided in about what I had been going through. In her message, she said that this is way too much drama, that she doesn't agree with my conclusions about what I have been going through, and that while she does believe I have been through something difficult, she just can't be a part of it anymore. She finished her message saying that she still considers me a friend and that she would like to still get together and hang out, provided that I never speak about such negative things with her.

Yes, I completely understood why she felt she needed to bow out. Even just hearing about my recent situation was surely terrifying, let alone living it! Even through my tears, I realized that if she were to truly accept what I had told her, it would mean that her whole belief system about our spiritual community would be shattered. While I understood why the truth would be too scary to face, I also felt angry at her offer to only be a fair-weather friend, to only be my friend as long as everything was kept positive and easy.

I was crushed. Not only had I been through something beyond traumatic, but there were so few people I could talk to about it, and so few people who would understand. As I stared vacantly at her message, I suddenly felt utterly alone and so much grief and sadness due to the people who had left my life because of this situation. I had posted a few references on social media about going through a psychic attack, and some of my energy healing colleagues had already unfriended and blocked me. I had even gone to a local metaphysical store to ask for advice, and the energy healer on duty literally would not speak to me or look at me once she heard about the problem I was trying to overcome. My mind reeled with feelings of rejection and despair. I felt so depressed all day, I could barely work. There were some projects I absolutely had to complete, involving content I was supposed to create and send to some of my students. After doing a couple of hours of self-care and having a good, therapeutic phone call with Sandra, I sat down to create a video for my students. Ironically, it was about my top seven favorite techniques for psychic self-defense. Immediately after I finished the recording, I uploaded the video to my computer and then to YouTube. When I was reviewing the video, I suddenly realized that about halfway through, the plasma-like entity appeared and was visible all the way to the end of the video!

What the hell?! I had done everything right, and that asshole entity was still in my house! I was pissed! After the video segment where I demonstrated how to burn sage for energy clearing, the dark figure began to take form as a large blob of pulsating white light behind my left side. On the wall behind me, there was a large, round, decorative mandala made of metal. Mouth agape, I scrutinized the video and saw energy flowing out of the center of the metal mandala, gradually forming into the plasma-like entity behind my left side.

In a rush, I sent the video to Raina and Sandra, and they both replied quickly, pointing out that they, too, could see the paranormal activity. Initially, I had not even thought to look for any entities in the video. I had erroneously thought my clearing methods had moved the entity issues out of my home, at least mostly. It was like the being was mocking me. "Hey, I'll show up in her video about psychic self-defense. And I'll show up right *after* she demonstrates the most popular energy clearing technique — burning sage." Funny...NOT funny! That night, I prayed even harder to receive the information needed to clear out the issue.

The next day, I was trying to upload the audio recording from my recent workshop on psychic protection and I kept getting 'error' messages. That had never happened before, but now it was suddenly happening with YouTube, Facebook, and my website. In the recent workshop, I had shared the story about what I had been recently going through. Apparently, 'something' out there did not want me to educate people about this topic.

I scrutinized the recent video even further, watching it over and over again. It was clear that the entity had come directly out of the center of the round, metal wall hanging. That wall hanging had apparently served as a portal and energy conduit. I thought about how I had followed Holly's advice a few days before recording the video. During a consultation with her, she had pointed out that I was doing lots of things right in regards to energetically protecting my home, but entities were still gaining easy access due to the fact that I had portals (energy doorways) in my home. Not only had the angel pin served as a portal, but Holly was able to psychically see that I had close to one hundred other portals in my home. I loved mandalas (a round geometric design) and dream catchers (a Native American craft). I had been collecting them over the years and decorating my home with them, yet they were all acting as spiritual portals. Based on Holly's recommendation, I had gone through my home and removed anything and everything that could possibly be a portal. I had removed every single potential portal, except I had left the round, metal mandala. I had purchased it for fifty dollars only a month ago, and I felt like I would be flushing my money down the toilet if I got rid of it so soon after buying it. I had left it on the wall, hoping it would be fine, not realizing that it was not only a portal, but it was a super-charged portal due to the fact that it was made of metal, a known conductor of energy. It had been the only portal I had not removed from my home, and the entity had traveled through it to gain access to me once again.

I stood up from my computer and walked straight to the wall hanging, took it off the wall, wrapped a piece of cloth around it covering and closing the energetic portal, and put it in a box in my garage. I then gathered my supplies and began burning frankincense, myrrh, copal, and dragon's blood tree resins. Walking around my home, I filled each room with the thick, aromatic smoke, saying prayers that all entities and negative energies be removed.

I continued this incense practice religiously every single day, and while the house felt energetically clear, I was still noticing indications that the plasma-like entity was still present. One night, I realized I had not seen my two cats in several hours. This was unusual because they were usually napping or playing somewhere near me. I checked every room and every closet and they were nowhere to be found. Finally, I opened the door to my attached garage, and there they both were, sitting at the bottom of the steps, with concerned looks on their faces, looking scared to come into the house. I walked down the stairs and tried to nudge them to come back into the house. Even when I pulled out the cat treats, they would not budge. Anyone with pets knows that animals are very in tune with energy. I believe their strange behavior was an indication that the entity had been bothering them in the house. Two days later, I had a personal transformation class at my home. I meditated and prayed before the class and also burned incense. I was very conscientious about making sure the house was one hundred percent clear before having students in my home. Yet, as soon as I began telling them about my recent psychic attack, the overhead lights began flashing on and off.

Crap! Was I ever going to get rid of this thing? I honestly was concerned that I would never be free from whatever this was, that perhaps it would be with me for the rest of my life. Perhaps I would need to completely stop doing my energy healing and teaching forever and even go into hiding. I knew that one thing was most certainly true. I needed to take some time off from my professional schedule to make sure this was completely cleared and to allow myself to heal emotionally. Not only was it extremely important to me that my clients and students have a completely safe environment, but I also realized that I was having symptoms of PTSD. I was having trouble sleeping, eating, and performing normal, daily tasks. The entire period of psychic attack had been really stressful, but the experience with the entity trying to tear my spirit out of my body had been utterly traumatic and horrifying. I announced to my students and clients that I would be taking some time off, and I focused on rest and self-care.

Raina, Sandra, and I scheduled a video conference call to discuss all that had been happening to each of us. Both Sandra and I expressed our feelings that this was happening to us for a reason — that we are supposed to somehow help people once we get through this — teach, support, remove entities. We were not sure yet exactly what we would be doing in the future, but we were both certain that our life purpose had changed and upgraded because of this.

After the video call, Raina and I went to a local vegan restaurant for lunch. We talked for a couple of hours, trying to get to the bottom of what was happening. Afterward, we stopped by one of our local metaphysical shops to browse and get more energy clearing supplies. I started chatting with one of the employees working behind the counter and followed my gut instinct to tell him what I had been going through. "Have you tried a Double-Action Reversible Candle?" he asked. Actually, I had not, but at this point, I was willing to try anything! I had always loved candle magick, but had never used Hoodoo practices in the past. To be honest, I had always kept certain spiritual practices at arm's length, even though I have respect for all paths. Namely, I had avoided any paths that I (correctly or erroneously) believed had practices of harming others via curses and hexes. I had always been open-minded about various spiritual paths and was open to learning about various pagan witchcraft practices while avoiding certain other magickal traditions completely. My mind clicked with the recognition that there were some rich spiritual traditions I had not yet allowed myself to delve into.

As I held the Hoodoo candle in my hand, I also realized that it would be important for me to study the practices of the entire spectrum, both the light and dark. Let's face it. Only having knowledge of the light makes me vulnerable to those who choose to use the dark against me. I personally will never be one to put hexes or curses on people, but I understood then how imperative it is that I know about dark magick, hex, and curse reversal.

(I'll be going through step-by-step candle burning instructions in the Lesson section of this chapter.)

Light a Candle for Me
As soon as I got home, I got right to work on using the candle. Setting the candle on a table top mirror, I wrote a prayer of intention on a slip of paper, held the paper in my hands for a few minutes as I prayed aloud, declaring my freedom from all psychic attack. Then, I slipped the paper between the candle and mirror and lit the candle with sacred intention.

The moment I lit the candle, I instantly saw an image of the white plasma entity being sucked out of my house. I looked out the window and clearly saw it right past the property line in the backyard, near the top of the powerline. The figure appeared to be struggling very hard to come back into my yard, but it was as though a tether was holding it back. I breathed a sigh of relief that the entity had been removed, and I returned my attention back to the candle. Gazing at the flame, I continued to pray for clearing and protection of not only this recent psychic attack, but for any and all psychic attack, large or small, that had been directed toward me in my lifetime. As I did so, I saw flashes of different people's faces and felt their feelings and intentions of jealousy and ill will being reversed away from me. I was amazed at how much psychic attack I had received through my lifetime. It was no wonder I had become so vulnerable!

I allowed the candle to burn for a couple of hours, but out of concern for fire safety, I went ahead and extinguished the candle before I went to bed, praying that the work I had begun would continue energetically until I lit the candle again the following day. Even though it was a seven-day candle that is intended to burn continuously, I instead only burned it when I was attending to it. Each day, for an hour up to several hours, I burned that candle and spent time in meditation and prayer, asking that any and all psychic attack, negative energies, and negative entities be removed completely, and disavowing any and all soul agreements that had made me a target in the first place. The entity did not return and all signs of psychic attack had dissipated completely. Over the next several weeks, I was able to focus on self-care and peace.

LESSON 11 – USING A REVERSAL CANDLE

Using a reversal candle is one of the most effective and simple techniques I have found to reverse psychic attack. A reversal candle (also called a reversible candle, or a double action reversible candle) is a two-color candle that is used to reverse, or send back, the energy that has been causing you trouble. Amazon.com, LuckyMojo.com, and your local metaphysical shops tend to carry these candles.

There is a long history of candles being used in various religious and spiritual practices throughout the world. Growing up Catholic, I remember lighting seven-day candles to pray for my loved ones. As an adult, I found a similar connection with pagan candle magick rituals. The particular technique I will be teaching you stems from Hoodoo practices. To be clear, I have a strong background in using candles to initiate powerful energetic change; however, I do not specialize in Hoodoo. In my own practices, I have found that simple is better, so I will be keeping my explanation fairly simple. (There are additional processes of using herbs and oils to dress the candle which we will not be going into here. If you want a more complex ritual, you will be able to easily find any add-on steps through a quick Google search.) Either way, I encourage you to take this technique and make it your own.

There are different varieties of reversal candles. For the sake of simplicity, I will be focusing primarily on one type (white/black) although I will be mentioning a few others as well. The reversal candle will have one color on top and one color on the bottom. Colors themselves have a particular vibration, and as such, each color of the candle will produce different energetic results when the candle is burned. The standard all-use candles for general psychic attack, hex, and curse are red on the top and black on the bottom. (Candles that are black on top and red on the bottom should not be confused with standard psychic attack reversal candles, as the black on top, red on the bottom candles are used specifically when the issues involve psychic attack on one's love life.) Candles that are white on top and black on the bottom are used to reverse psychic attacks where entities are involved. White and black candles are the ones I use the most because they are effective in clearing out general psychic attack (negative energy sent your way) as well as entity interference. Reversal candles that are green on top and black on the bottom are used when the psychic attack has impacted your finances.

If you are not sure which one you need, I suggest the white/black candle because it will help with general psychic attack and also clear out any entities (known or unknown) that may be involved in the situation. If you are completely positive there are no entities involved, go ahead and use a red and black candle. Follow your inner guidance on which one is best for you at this time. If, for some reason, you are not able to obtain an actual reversal candle, you can use two regular candles (tapers or votives), one of each color, and light them at the same time while doing the reversal candle steps. I have found that an actual reversal candle seems to work much better in this process, so try to obtain one if you can.

Common Types of Reversal Candles:

Red/Black (red on top, black on bottom) — used for general psychic attack, hex, or curse

Black/Red (black on top, red on bottom) — used for psychic attack relating to love life

White/Black (white on top, black on bottom) — used for psychic attack including entity activity

Green/Black (green on top, black on bottom) — used for psychic attack impacting finances

From here on out, I will be focusing on the white/black reversal candles, but know that you can apply the concepts and procedures to the other candles as you choose. When working with a white and black candle, white removes and breaks the bond, while black protects you and returns the energy to the sender. Whether the psychic attack was intentionally or unintentionally sent by a person, the negative energy they have sent will leave you and be returned to them. If you are uncomfortable with this, you can set the intention that the negative energy will simply leave you and go out into the universe to be recycled and healed. Psychic attacks that are directly initiated by an entity (or the Dark Forces in general) will be removed from you and the entities will not be permitted to return.

Supplies:

- Pen and paper
- Small mirror for your tabletop
- Reversal candle (color and type depending on your needs)
- Lighter wand

Process:

Step 1: On a piece of paper, in your own words and in your own handwriting, write a declaration:

[Your name on top]
I, (state your name), now reverse and release any and all negative energy cords, entity attachments, implants, negative thought-forms, possession, oppression, infestation by entities, black magick, curses, hexes, psychic attack, evil eye, mind control, energies of evil, chaos, drama, jealousy, anger, resentment, and confusion. I disavow any and all non-beneficial agreements or contracts in this lifetime, past lives, future lives, parallel lifetimes, in all dimensions and realities now and forever. I now reverse, release, and disavow any and all non-beneficial energies, contracts, or agreements that may be cloaked or sealed with black magick or any other means. All karma is healed and complete. All non-beneficial energies are reversed now and forever, and my life returns to peace, prosperity, harmony, and health. And so it is. Amen.

Step 2: Call on God and the angels [and whoever you pray to for assistance.] Read the declaration with conviction. Then carefully fold the paper several times.

Step 3: Place mirror, face up, on the table top.

Step 4: Place the folded piece of paper on top of mirror.

Step 5: Place candle on top of paper/mirror.

Step 6: Say a prayer as you light the candle.

Step 7: Sit and watch the candle for a while and pray/meditate.

Always attend to the candle. When you are ready to blow it out, ask that a guardian angel watch over the candle and keep the power of the candle going strong, even when it is not lit. Light the candle every single day for as long as you can attend to it. Do not miss a day because it is important to keep the energy going.

CHAPTER 12 - DIVINE DOWNLOAD

My sleep was still pretty messed up. Most nights I would stay up late and still have trouble falling asleep by two or three in the morning. I knew that a part of me was still afraid to go to sleep, that I could be attacked while I slept, even though there were no indications of remaining entity activity. Everything appeared to be totally clear of psychic attack since I had begun using the reversal candle ten days prior.

I was going through a period of depression and PTSD, yet at the same time, I could sense very powerful shifts of personal and spiritual transformation within me. I struggled with feelings of sadness and isolation, feeling very alone that there were so few people who understood what had happened to me. Not only had my dear friend Debbie pushed me away, but a number of 'love and light' spiritual colleagues had unfriended and blocked me on Facebook and would no longer speak to me.

I even had a totally bizarre experience of overt shunning when I visited a local metaphysical shop. When I arrived at the shop, I wandered around for a bit looking at the merchandise. The woman on duty doing energy healing sessions that day was standing at the back of the shop. We had met on one previous occasion, and considering her a colleague, I went over to say hello.

"Hi there! How are you today?" I asked cheerfully.

The woman stood with her back straight as a board, staring upward, her face emotionless, and saying nothing.

I continued with friendliness, "I'm Maya. Do you remember me? We chatted before."

She still stared upward, clearly refusing to look at me, and said through clenched teeth, "Yes, I remember you, and I want nothing to do with you."

"Okay, I'm sorry you feel that way."

I finished my shopping and left.

I knew in my gut that there were many other people in the world who had suffered through terrifying psychic attack experiences, and I was also pretty sure that most of them had also encountered a lack of support. My experience at the metaphysical shop only served to solidify my inner calling to create support systems for those who have gone through this kind of trauma.

Who's the Victim Here?
The next day, I had a phone call with my former church youth group leader, Victoria, from when I was in high school. I had been a very religious and spiritual teen and had had numerous mystical visions during that time. My hope was that Victoria would be able to offer some spiritual insights or perhaps be able to help me connect with a priest within the Catholic Church who would be willing to talk with me about spiritual

warfare.

I shared my entire story with Victoria, and her immediate response was this, "I am not in any way trying to victim blame here, but I want to ask you, what red flags might you have missed? How could you have had better discernment?"

Wow, she actually was victim blaming. She had nothing to discuss with me about spiritual warfare. The whole conversation continued with her emphasis that I should have had better judgment. The conversation overall was pleasant and courteous, and I knew she meant well. But, I was really starting to get angry and fed up with the implications of personal fault I was encountering.

The fact was, I had already been using such a high level of discernment around the time of the recent attack that I would not go to most energy healers or spiritual events in town, because either they did not match my level of integrity, or they did not match the vibration that I had chosen for myself. And yet, even though I was basically living like a hermit, exceedingly careful who I would allow into my inner circle, there were still some very skilled imposters who flew undetected below my radar. These are people who put on a very convincing image of being love and light, and who are very highly regarded in the community. They have fooled a lot of people, and they continue to do so even today.

After talking with Victoria, I was deeply pondering the

whole unsupportive victim blaming pattern that seemed to be so prevalent. I thought up an imaginary scenario that could happen in real life, an event that could illustrate a parallel to the type of psychic attack situation I went through. Let's say there was a woman, we'll call her Kay. She asks all her friends what doctor they recommend. They all rave about Dr. Smith, so she calls his office and makes an appointment. He seems really nice and like he really knows what he is talking about. She schedules follow-up appointments because her health issues are not yet resolved. At one of these appointments, he makes sexual advances toward her and touches her inappropriately during an exam. She feels angry and violated, emotionally distraught, and traumatized by what happened. She reports the incident to the authorities. She goes to her friends for support, and they say things like:

"Why didn't you have better discernment?"
"I don't agree with your interpretation of what happened."
"I can't support you through this. It's just too negative."
"Like energy attracts like, so there must have been some low vibration energy within you that attracted this situation."
People said those exact things to me, by the way. And victims of crime, assault, abuse, illness, and terrible circumstances are victim blamed every day, whether the assault is of this earth or is of a spiritual nature. Trauma, whatever the cause, is difficult enough without accusing the victim or making them feel complicit.

As I pondered my conversation with Victoria and the whole dysfunctional issue with victim blaming in our culture, I shuffled my angel card deck and pulled a card for inspiration. It was the Archangel Michael card. This was so apt, because Archangel Michael is a powerful kick ass angel of strength and protection who assists with spiritual warfare. I took a deep breath and could feel some of my strength returning.

Over the next couple of weeks, I took time to rest, recover, and recharge, and found that the respite helped tremendously. Now that all aspects of the psychic attack had been cleared, I was in a state of deep gratitude for making it through everything. I felt very strongly that I did not want to go through anything like that ever again! And yet, I was feeling so grateful for everything I had learned and how the situation had helped me find aspects of my inner strength I never knew I had. This was a situation that really changed me, deepened me, and strengthened me in ways I cannot even describe. I was seeing the world differently than I had before, but it was good to have my eyes opened to the truth.

I sat at my personal altar, a coffee table draped with a deep blue chiffon cloth with gold edging. My altar reflected my eclectic beliefs. There were candles, sage, mala beads, a rosary, seashells, feathers, crystals, and statues of Mother Mary, Kuan Yin, Lakshmi, and Archangel Michael. I prayed for peace on earth for all sentient beings. I prayed to be given the knowledge of how to protect myself from psychic attack *before* it happens. I asked to be shown and taught what *does* work so I could share this information with others. I took a few slow deep breaths and felt the answers flow through me. I picked up my pen and wrote in my journal.

To reduce vulnerability to psychic attack:

1. Embark on a lifelong journey to work on personal healing and transformation. Heal all that would make you energetically vulnerable to psychic attack, including tears, holes, damage to aura, negative soul contracts, karma, contributing beliefs, victim-consciousness, passiveness and lack of empowerment, and more. (In addition, if any mental health, addiction, or physical health issues are present, the person needs to seek professional medical support for these.)

2. Have a daily spiritual practice which helps keep your energy clear, grounded, and strong, and keeps you in touch with Divine Source and your spiritual team (guides and guardian angels, etc.).

3. For daily maintenance, engage in a daily clearing/release/reversal of all psychic attack (minor or major), energy cords, non-beneficial energy, entity attachments, etc.

After receiving this information, I continued to receive a flow of ongoing divine downloads and sacred visions over the next few months and beyond. People began coming to me with questions about psychic protection and spirituality, and I would speak at length about things that I somehow knew, that I had never learned from books or working with any teachers. Every day, I was working on the three items in the list above, working on healing anything that had made me vulnerable to psychic attack, nurturing my relationship with God and my guardian angels, and practicing a daily clearing routine.

During that time, new clients began contacting me out of the blue, people who were having issues with psychic attack and entity attachment. In the past, I would have outright avoided working with these types of cases (because I was afraid!), but I knew in my bones that I was now being called to help these people. Admittedly, I felt a healthy dose of trepidation when I worked with my first couple of clients with severe psychic protection issues. What if I came under attack as a result of working with these clients? But, my techniques worked, and the new knowledge and skills I had received via divine download continued to be effective. My confidence and knowledge continued to grow each day.

I had vowed to create a support group once I got through my psychic attack, and I did just that. I created a free Facebook group where people from all over the world could gather in a safe, sacred space, and I offered a free online class once per month, too. There was no turning back. I could not NOT do this work.

As I began embarking on this new path, I still felt like I was going around in circles and racking my brain. I told Raina and Sandra that I wondered if we would ever truly know all of the answers about what happened to us. I realized that I had still been looking to other spiritual healers and psychics to explain this unusual series of events, but these people did not have the answers I was seeking. The answers were already within me.

When I finally allowed myself to listen to my inner knowing about what happened, I could finally see that I had in fact experienced a quadruple-layered psychic attack. Beginning at the end of April, Jeffrey started sending psychic attacks to me and others, which was when some of the people connected with his work had expressed concern that Jeffrey had a demonic attachment. The attacks I received were fairly mild (in retrospect) and included nightmares, troubling emotions, anxiety, feelings of negative energy looming, as well as some drama and rumors thrown into the mix.

The second layer started for me when things heated up with Anne. Having shown a pattern of power struggles, dabbling with magick, and trying to prove that she was more powerful than me, I believe she did black magick to manipulate my energy and try to put me in my place. As I tuned in intuitively, I could see a clear image of her doing spell work against me. She was the one who sent the energy of confusion, the all-seeing ravens, and the eerie feeling of being watched.

The third layer began when I had first contact with Darlene. Things went really crazy a few weeks later when I attended her angel healing group and purchased the angel pin and book, thus unknowingly allowing direct access for entity attack and ongoing spiritual surveillance. Occurrences of missing time, bends in reality, seeing odd spiritual beings, and questioning my sanity were all results of being in direct contact with Darlene's false light entity. In addition, the fact that there were three layers of attack occurring simultaneously made it easier for Jeffrey's demon to gain direct access to me and to assault me that night while I was in bed.

After that, there were ongoing demonic attacks and spiritual encounters that I am now sure were thoughtforms, not actual demons. Thoughtforms can be just as powerful and damaging as actual entities. These thoughtform attacks were initiated by Darlene's entity and continued daily until the moment I put the angel pin and book away in my garage.

The dark being working through Darlene is known as a false light being, an imposter entity, a shapeshifter, a djinn. It has many people convinced that it is a group of angels, when in fact it is one single dark entity. This false light being sucks Darlene's life force energy and ultimately uses her as a means to hook into many unsuspecting clients and students, causing psychic attack for these people and feeding off their energy.

The fourth layer of the attack occurred when I came under direct attack from Darlene's entity. When I tried to speak up and warn some of the individuals that were a part of this being's feeding web, the entity appeared firsthand and tried to tear my soul out of my body. It's goal? To take me down or get me to back down.

What I came to understand was that a major psychic attack can begin with a minor psychic attack. Once you are weakened, even just a tiny bit, the next wave can hit more easily. In my case, there were four waves. It is a miracle I survived.

I do believe that while this horrific quadruple-layer psychic attack was caused by the Dark Forces, the whole scenario was allowed to occur because I was supposed to be exposed to this firsthand experience and knowledge. Let me be clear: This situation was horrible and I do not wish it upon anyone! But, reading a book or attending a workshop could never give me the knowledge and conviction I now have. This has literally shifted the trajectory of my life's work and my life as a whole. Without this life-jarring experience, I could not have written this book.

LESSON 12 – THE ILLUSION MATRIX

In this lesson, I'll be discussing the Illusion Matrix, what it is, and how it is having an impact in our world today. The Illusion Matrix is a network of false light beings that serve the dark agenda hidden within the realm that I call the Dark Web.

When I speak of the dark agenda, I am referring to the evil forces that exist in our reality. Whether you want to think of these evil forces as demons, djinn, alien reptilians, archons, or what have you, the end result is still the same. These dark beings work to stir up emotional suffering (depression, anxiety, hatred, rage, greed, etc.) so that they can feed off of the loosh, the energy that is created through the suffering of sentient beings. To confuse matters, these evil beings also feed off of the energy of adoration and worship, which is one reason so many of them choose to take on a false appearance as light beings. There are many different types of spiritual beings that work within the dark agenda, but defining all of them would go beyond the scope of this book. Suffice it to say that these negative forces work against the highest good of the human race and all beings on our planet.

The Dark Forces have two basic approaches for driving down the vibration of the human race. The first is when dark entities appear as the dark beings they truly are. In this state, they can directly attack a human through psychic attack, entity attachment, possession, or infestation of a home. They can attach to a person and encourage them into evil acts such as homicide, mass shooting, pedophilia, and other horrific behavior. They can connect with a person who has a confused moral compass and encourage them to willingly serve the Dark Forces. And the list goes on.

The second approach is when dark entities disguise themselves as light beings—as loved ones, angels, ascended masters, benevolent aliens, etc. This vast network of imposter entities is what I called the Illusion Matrix. What is the purpose of the Illusion Matrix? The Dark Forces are able to get much more traction by preying upon not only those who are susceptible to darkness, but also those who are drawn to goodness and light.

The Illusion Matrix is the perfect smokescreen and the most effective way the dark forces can infiltrate spiritual communities so easily. The Illusion Matrix has infiltrated the majority (about 90%) of New Age/spiritual/metaphysical communities all over the world. I felt so much sadness and despair when I was shown this. To be clear, this is not just happening in my own local community. It is happening everywhere.

What do I mean when I say that the Illusion Matrix has infiltrated the New Age community? I mean that people are channeling messages and freely working with spirit guides, so-called angels, and supposed ascended beings that they genuinely believe are light beings, but that are in actuality dark beings disguised as light. They are unknowingly working with imposter entities.

One reason the Dark Forces have been so effective at this is that, through this network of false light channelings, they have spread the spiritual belief that we should not practice discernment or healthy boundaries. When messages are channeled through false light beings, they are filled with encouraging, loving, inspiring teachings mixed with a few threads of untruth. In this way, the messages are easily received and readily believed by unsuspecting followers. Their most effective lies are those mixed with convincing, lovely truths.

And so, the false teachings are inserted to manipulate the masses. The belief that we are all one, therefore, there is no need to protect yourself or have boundaries, has become so prevalent and even dogmatic, that if someone steps outside of that teaching to practice boundaries, they are often shamed and shunned by spiritual followers who have been brainwashed by the false teachings. This allows the cycle to continue, creating fewer people who will question whether a spiritual being is truly who or what they say they are.

Another very prevalent false teaching is the belief that since everything was created by God, that means that all beings in existence are positive and good. The supposition, therefore, is that evil entities do not exist, that Dark Forces do not exist, and therefore, it is completely safe to open yourself up completely to connect with any and all energies in the Universe. A similar false teaching is that everything is simply energy, therefore, there is no good or bad within the

Universe; it's simply neutral energy. With these false teachings, followers are unknowingly yet willingly opening themselves up to parasitic relationships with the Dark Forces. By convincing the masses that they do not exist, members of the Dark Web can easily prey upon countless non-resistant victims.

Those who have disturbing experiences with dark entities are told that these beings do not exist, and that it was just a projection of their own inner shadow, some unhealed aspect from deep within themselves. In essence, anyone who tries to speak up is told it is all in their head. The false channeled teachings supporting lack of boundaries and the denial of Dark Forces are followed as dogmatic truth and anyone who does not follow the distorted dogma is told they are being "fear based." And so, the false channeled teachings are mixed with shunning and peer pressure to follow the mass beliefs, beliefs that were initiated by members of the Dark Web. It is all one big puppet show.

One of my very sweet colleagues used to post comments on my Facebook page quite often, insisting that my practice of healthy boundaries was anti-oneness and anti-love. Her husband often posted similar comments and claimed that both Gandhi and Martin Luther King, Jr were appearing to him and telling him that I should stop teaching about boundaries and psychic protection. The colleague even encouraged her husband to send me a video that included false light channelings. The video literally had a written message at the beginning that said, "There is no need to protect yourself." The video began with strange noises and frequencies and then continued with a voice speaking an alien language. After a few moments, I quickly realized it was a mind control video, so I quickly clicked it off. I messaged the colleague and her husband and told them if they ever sent me a video like this again, I would block them.

In addition to false light channelings, spiritual communities are tapped into through the use of 'spiritual anesthetic.' When spiritual seekers attend one-on-one client sessions or group events which have been infiltrated by the false light agenda, these participants are flooded with feelings of anesthetizing euphoria and even experiences of illusory healing to distract them as negative entities plug into them. Participants assume that these blissed-out states are indicative of a positive spiritual experience, but in actuality, these states are initiated by false light entities as they actively plug energy cords into the participants. Every time false light entities plug into wide open, non-resistant spiritual seekers, the Illusion Matrix grows even more in power, size, and influence.

The problem is, the Illusion Matrix is so embedded that it is nearly impossible for people to see when they are inside the web. I have found through experience that, most of the time, it is ineffective to directly try to help someone who is caught in the imposter web. The person simply cannot see how they are trapped, and they will often become defensive and hostile if you try to describe these facts to them. The result is that the imposter entities working with them pull them in even deeper. Their vision is so obscured by the matrix that it is hard for them to see the truth. This is why my own approach is through teaching and writing, and not through trying to convince individuals who are already caught in the Illusion. Through teaching and writing, those who are ready can receive the information and integrate it in whatever way is best for them. I have also found that when people proactively learn the truth about the Illusion Matrix, they are more likely to have the spiritual tools necessary to avoid getting hooked in.

So, how do you avoid getting hooked into the Illusion Matrix? By being informed. By questioning everything, while also having an open mind. By being extremely conscious of every intention, from every person and every spiritual being, even if they say they are of the light, even if they have thousands and thousands of followers. By being cautious with *all* guides, teachers, and healers (both physical and spiritual)—even me! True teachers of the light will not be bothered or offended by being questioned or tested. They will be glad you are using strong discernment!

All physical guides, teachers, and healers are human beings, and as such, they are not always perfect. There is a difference between being a flawed human and being controlled by Dark Forces, knowingly or unknowingly. Through using knowledgeable judgment, you will learn to see the difference.

When it comes to spiritual guides, you will learn to distinguish between what is false light and what is truly coming from Divine Source, true light. False light will often seem a bit off with the feeling that something is not quite right. False light can be very convincing! It is best to err on the side of caution when you are not sure.

As a clairvoyant, I see false light as being too bright, so bright that it hurts my eyes, as though it is trying to overcompensate. I have observed that this extra brightness tends to make spiritual seekers subconsciously attracted to the light. These seekers are truly yearning for Divine light, and they unknowingly connect with false light because it is so shiny and attractive.

Over the years, I have noticed a glow of light around healers and teachers who are controlled by false light entities. (Before I knew any better, I used to be drawn to it because I thought it meant these people were extra holy.) This is essentially an energetic 'glamour' used by false light entities to draw in spiritual seekers. I have also noticed that their eyes will often have an unusual opalescent quality. Recently, I dropped in to say hello to a colleague I had not seen in several months. I gasped when I saw his eyes. I knew he was someone who did not have very good judgment and that he had been spending a lot of time with people infested with false light entities. In hindsight, I was not surprised to see the significant change in his eyes and energy.

I have so much love, empathy, and compassion for those who are plugged into the Illusion Matrix—those who are unknowingly working with imposter entities. Most of them have no idea what is really happening and they are being controlled by the very clever Dark

Forces. The whole Illusion Matrix is a complex and interwoven network that blows my mind every time I look at it. It is a web of false light entities connected to people connected to more false light entities connected to more people. The whole purpose is to feed off of human energy and to keep humanity misled and distracted with false teachings.

Let me be clear. Even if your heart is filled with love and light, you can still be a target of the Dark Forces. In fact, *because* your heart is filled with love and light, this in itself can make you a target. I don't say this to scare you. I say it to snap you into reality. Those who are most afraid to face the dark head on, those who prefer to avoid anything uncomfortable and cling to the belief that darkness does not exist, those are the ones who are most often targeted by false light beings. Those are the ones who most often get trapped in the Illusion Matrix.

Do not be afraid to see the truth. You are so much stronger than you think. You can be a true lightworker, a true warrior of the light, a true seer of truth. You are capable of cutting through illusion, of slicing through the darkness, of bringing more authentic light and healing into this world. If you feel overwhelmed at the state of our spiritual reality, just know this: True bravery is seeing the truth of darkness and choosing to stand up anyway to live your life with joy, compassion, and love, and to shine your light even brighter despite it all.

Appendix: Additional Resources

Sign up for Maya's email newsletter at

www.PsychicProtectionSanctuary.com to find out about new books, programs, upcoming events, and more.

Free Bonus Content

Checklist: Are You Under Psychic Attack?

Go to www.PsychicProtectionSanctuary.com and enter your email address to receive this bonus content.

This comprehensive checklist will help you determine if you are under psychic attack and the severity of that attack. Discover some of the lesser-known symptoms of negative spiritual interference so you can get a better grasp of your situation.

YouTube Channel

Subscribe to the Psychic Protection Sanctuary YouTube channel for more free content.

Free Facebook Group

Connect with Maya Zahira and others like you within this free private online group available to those who answer the three membership questions prompted when you request to join. Go to Facebook and search for the following group: "Psychic Protection Sanctuary with Maya Zahira ~ Psychic Attack Support."

Group Energy Clearing with Maya Zahira

A donation-based online membership program where you can receive powerful, daily energy clearing within a group setting. Join anytime. Sign up at www.PsychicProtectionSanctuary.com.

Maya Zahira's Online
Spiritual Empowerment Academy

This is Maya's premium flagship program and is a culmination of her many years of work helping others with spiritual development and psychic self-defense.

If you are dealing with....

- A psychic attack, curse, or other negative spiritual interference
- Exposure to unwanted dark forces or spiritual warfare
- Spirit attachment or entity harassment
- Disentangling from an abusive spiritual teacher, healer, or dark shaman
- Or, the challenges of being a spiritually-targeted individual....

You need Spiritual Empowerment Academy!

"What first inspired me to join Maya's program was her authenticity and connection to Spirit. I have enjoyed learning from the program because her teaching is grounded, easy to follow, and the techniques are practical. She GENUINELY cares about her students and helps us achieve our potential through personalized spiritual healing and intuitive guidance. The best part, in my opinion, is the safe, loving, and sacred community space passionately nurtured by Maya." S.F., Nebraska

Visit www.PsychicProtectionSanctuary.com to apply.

Other Books by Maya Zahira

Visit www.PsychicProtectionSanctuary.com and sign up for the email newsletter to receive updates on future books.

The Psychic Attack Sourcebook: Understanding and Surviving the Unimaginable

Psychic attack can happen to anyone, and it is more common than most would like to imagine. Unwanted paranormal encounters, black magick, ancestral curses, entity harassment, possession, and more can wreak havoc on the life of a targeted individual. Without the right information and support, the victim can suffer for years, struggling to overcome the nightmare of ongoing spiritual warfare.

Within the pages of this book, you will learn the secrets and tactics the Dark Forces do not want you to know. Gain the upper hand as you master tangible steps to help guide you on your journey to reclaim your energy from these malevolent powers. The better armed you are in these practices, the less vulnerable you will be to negative spiritual influences.

"This is THE most important book on psychic attack.... This book exposes the underbelly of what the Dark Forces are really up to and gives actionable steps on how to defeat them."

MCJ, Colorado, spiritual warfare survivor

Available in paperback and Kindle at Amazon.com.

Printed in Poland
by Amazon Fulfillment
Poland Sp. z o.o., Wrocław

24960956R00177